Hegemony and Counter-Hegemony

Marxism, Capitalism and their Relation to Sexism, Racism, Nationalism and Authoritarianism

Lenny Flank

Red and Black Publishers, St Petersburg, Florida, 2007

Publishers Cataloging in Publication Data –

Flank, Lenny, 1961-

   Hegemony and Counter-Hegemony: Marxism, Capitalism, and Their Relation to Sexism, Racism, Nationalism and Authoritarianism/Lenny Flank

   p. cm.

   ISBN: 978-0-9791813-7-5

1. Marxism. 2. Social Movements – United States. 2. Political Participation – United States

I. Title

HN65 .F53 2007

303.48   LCCN: 2007932146

Red and Black Publishers, PO Box 7542, St Petersburg, Florida, 33734

Contact us at: info@RedandBlackPublishers.com

CONTENTS

Preface

This book has two distinct purposes. The first is to present a radical critique of the existing social order in its various facets. Since the book is aimed primarily at radical activists, I have assumed that the reader has at least a passing acquaintance with the social movements and points of view being discussed here.

On the other hand, this book is intended as a critique of the prevailing "Marxist-Leninist" theory of social revolution, from the point of view of left-wing Marxism. It is my belief that the traditional "Communist" point of view which currently dominates the Left is incapable of providing a useful framework for examining existing society, and that a broader, more inclusive point of view must be adopted by radicals everywhere.

This is not a book for academics, for those who are content to analyze, dialecticalize and pontificate. This book is intended for activists — for those who are actively organizing people to change the actual circumstances under which we live. Although I have found it necessary to present and critique the theoretical presumptions under which many modern revolutionaries operate, this book is an attempt to begin a serious debate about revolutionary tactics and actions, not ideology or theory.

I am sorry that the book presents as many quotations from the Marxist sources as it does. This was not done because I consider the Marxist canon to be the ultimate authority on everything—quite the opposite. The quotations are simply an attempt to avoid pointless pedantic arguments over "what Marx really said". And, in order not to turn the book into a research project or theoretical treatise, I have not burdened the reader with endless source notes and explanatory footnotes. Marx's works are widely enough available that researchers should have no problem finding them.

I have chosen the viewpoint of left-wing Marxism or council communism because it is the point of view that has the greatest effect on my own personal position, as a white, straight male worker living in the United States. While I can (and do) give my support to other social justice movements, I have chosen to focus my efforts on the struggle which I know best and can fight most effectively. I expect that other activists with different situations will do the same. All I ask is that we coordinate our efforts together against our mutual enemy.

Introduction

To most people, the terms "Marxism", "Communism" and "Marxism-Leninism" are synonymous. These terms have been used interchangeably to refer to a specific set of social, economic and political doctrines, a set of doctrines that draws from theorists as diverse as Karl Marx, Vladimir Ilyich Lenin, Leon Trotsky, Mao Zedong, Fidel Castro, and Che Guevara. In the United States, the label "Marxist" has been applied to organizations as different from each other as the Communist Party USA, the Socialist Worker's Party, the Revolutionary Communist Party, the Progressive Labor Party, and the Spartacist League.

All of these people and parties come from the Leninist tradition, which completely dominated Marxist thought from the Bolshevik Revolution in 1917 until the collapse of the Communist Bloc in the 1990's. The Bolshevik tradition has become so inextricably intertwined with radical socialism that even today, when most people speak of "Marxism", they are actually referring to the doctrines of Leninism.

In the years after the Bolshevik Revolution, however, a completely different trend of thought had briefly flowered before succumbing to the Leninist purges. This tradition, known as "council communism", also traced its precepts to the philosophical outlooks of Karl Marx, but found itself in bitter opposition to the disciplined, centralized Leninists. By the time of the Second World War, the council communist movement had been all but eliminated, and the Leninists reigned supreme.

Today, after the collapse of the Soviet Union and its empire, we can see that the Leninist critique of industrial society is incomplete as well as a failure. Economics is not the sole determinant of social relationships, as the Leninists claim. Any social mode of production must not only produce and distribute the economic means of existence, but also all of the various social institutions and relationships which make up the social framework. All modes of production must determine, not only how the needs of life are produced (economics), but also how different members of society relate to each other and to other societies (race, sexual roles, religion, ethnicity, nation, gender, etc.), and the form of the power and authority structures which hold this social framework in place (law, police, state, education, etc.).

Taken together, all of these various social constructions make up the total mode of production, as well as the means by which the ruling elites maintain and protect their positions of privilege. The council communist school of Marxism refers to this vast interconnecting web of social relationships as a "hegemony".

Radical critics have examined modern industrial society from a number of different points of reference, with each critique emphasizing the particular concerns of the criticizer. Radical feminists, for example, view society in terms of patriarchy—the subordination of women to men—and thus use "sexism" as a means to explain human society. Gay and lesbian activists frame their critiques in terms of sexuality and sexual roles. Radical environmentalists focus their attention on the relationship between industrial society and its surroundings. African-American, Latino, Native American and other activists use racial and national viewpoints to examine social relationships.

Anarchists see society through the lens of power and authority structures, and thus focus their point of view on an anti-authoritarian critique of the state. Traditional Marxists and Leninists focus on the economy, and conclude that economic class factors determine the structure of society.

In reality, however, it can be seen that the dividing lines between these outlooks are blurry, and that each of these factors — economy, authority, race, sexuality, nation and gender — interact with each other to form modern industrial society. In every sphere of bourgeois society, these "sub-structures" reinforce and reproduce each other. Marx referred to the interaction of these interpenetrating entities as a "dialectic"; a dialectical relationship is one on which both elements co-determine each other through simultaneous interaction. Marx concluded that human society interacts with itself in a dialectical way.

Towards the end of his life, Marx intended to write a series of books examining the dialectical roles of non-economic factors in the reproduction of bourgeois society. Unfortunately, he died before that work could be completed. *Hegemony and Counter-Hegemony* is an attempt to begin a new analysis in this direction.

However, as Marx wrote, it is not enough to interpret and understand the world; the point is to change it. We cannot change the existing social order, though, unless we first understand how it protects and reproduces itself, and how it maintains its position of hegemony.

Overtly repressive societies such as Nazi Germany or the Soviet Union depend upon blunt police force and military power to maintain their social relationships. Challenges to the existing social structure are simply hunted down and liquidated.

In modern bourgeois society, however, the use of armed force is unleashed only in the rarest of instances, after all other methods have failed. One of the most remarkable things about capitalism has been its ability to compel people, without using overt force or repression, to conform to the social roles which allow the bourgeois class to exist and prosper. If the bourgeois mode of production is a dictatorship, it certainly appears to be a benevolent one.

The concept of "hegemony" explains this ability to reproduce unequal social relationships without resorting to physical coercion. Through a series of intertwining social relationships, bourgeois society is able to maintain the conditions for its existence and to reproduce these conditions.

The purpose of this book, then, is to examine this interconnecting web of social relationships from the points of view of its most prominent critics—feminists, anti-racists and national activists, environmentalists, gay and lesbian activists, anarchists, and socialists. Together, these outlooks provide a critique of bourgeois hegemony. They also provide clues as to how this hegemony can be broken, and how new, egalitarian, social relationships can be put in its place.

The bourgeois social order is thus like a hydra, a many-headed dragon. Try to cut off one head, and the others will kill you. The only way to kill the beast is to cut off all of its heads at once. In this book, we examine the capitalist beast's heads one at a time, in order to determine how best to lay the dragon in its grave.

Leninism

Before we can look to a new revolutionary way of studying bourgeois social structures, we must examine and understand the mistakes made by the old ways. In particular, we must understand the inherent limitations of the currently dominant version of "Marxism". Most modern Marxist groups refer to their outlook as "dialectical materialism" or "historical materialism" (both terms which Marx himself never used). The starting point of this outlook, they say, comes from a passage written by Marx himself:

> The materialist conception of history starts from the proposition that the production of the means to support human life and, next to production, the exchange of things produced, is the basis of all social structure; that in every society that has appeared in history, the manner in which wealth is distributed and society divided into classes or orders is dependent upon what is produced, how it is produced, and how the products are exchanged. From this point of view the final causes of all social changes and revolutions are to be sought, not in men's brains, not in men's better insights into eternal truth and justice, but in changes in the modes of production and exchange. They are to be sought not in the philosophy but in the economics of each particular epoch.

Through his study of political economy, Marx came to conclude that the basic structure of any human society was made up of the various institutions and relationships that were necessary for the reproduction of life and for the replication of social relationships. As both Marx and Engels point out, this "mode of production" should not be thought of in mere economic terms:

> This mode of production must not be considered simply as being the reproduction of the physical existence of individuals. Rather, it is a definite form of activity of these individuals, a definite mode of life on their part.

> This, again, is of a two-fold character. On the one side, the production of the means of existence, of articles of food and clothing, dwelling, and of the tools necessary for that production; on the other side, the production of human beings themselves, the propagation of the species. The social organization under which the people of a particular historical epoch and a particular country live is determined by both kinds of production.

> The form of intercourse determined by the existing productive forces at all previous historical stages, and in its turn determining them, is civil society... Civil society embraces the whole material intercourse of individuals within a definite stage of development of productive forces.

The social and political relationships that make up this mode of living were, Marx concluded, themselves based upon an interaction with existing circumstances:

> The social structure and the state are continually evolving out of the life-process of definite individuals, but of individuals not as they appear in their own or other people's imaginations, but as they really are, i.e., as they operate, produce materially and hence as they work under definite material limits, presuppositions and conditions independent of their will.

Social and political relationships are, moreover, controlled and dominated by the same class that has control of the economy (and vice versa). The social conventions of law, government, philosophy, morality and religion serve not simply to support and safeguard the economic structures which produce wealth for society, but also as a means whereby the ruling class protects its position of privilege within these existing relationships.

After Marx's death, his thought was adopted and codified by a group of German socialists who formed a new international organization to propagate them, the Second International. The theorists of the Second International in turn modified the dialectical nature of Marxism, and began to refer to it as a "science" which could explain and predict the motions of human society. Marxism was transformed into a series of "natural laws" which, theorists claimed, made the introduction of socialism a historical inevitability, regardless of human intentions or actions.

The Marxist-Leninists, in their Third International, and the Trotskyists, in their Fourth International, took this notion of "economic determinism" to its logical conclusion. The Leninists asserted that (1) Marxism describes the natural laws which govern the development of human society, (2) trained Marxist-Leninists are able to interpret these laws and thus to predict the future development of that society, and therefore (3) the party of trained Marxist-Leninists should be allowed to rule over that society to insure that it is guided, according to these natural laws, down the inevitable path to socialism.

Leninist theory is most often presented in the form of the "base—superstructure" network. According to this view, the economic relationships of society are the "base" upon which that society is founded, and all other social relationships (sexual, familial, racial, national) are merely a "superstructure" which reflects this economic base. Prevailing economic conditions, these "economic determinists" assert, form the basis of religious, familial, legal, ethical and other social relationships, and these non-economic structures can only be altered through changes in the economic base. As Stalin put it, "Every base has a superstructure corresponding to it. . . If the base changes or is eliminated, then following this its superstructure changes or is eliminated; if a new base arises, then following this a superstructure arises corresponding to it."

According to this conception, then, humans are mere products of their economic circumstances, and all human thoughts and actions are mere reflections of economic conditions. Humans are *Homo economicus*, directed by the impersonal laws of economic development.

The Leninist "base — superstructure" paradigm is, however, incomplete and cannot describe bourgeois society as a whole. It focuses narrowly on the effects of economic relationships upon humans without recognizing that human relationships have a profound impact upon economic structures.

Marx never made the mistake of asserting that economic relationships were the sole determining factor in bourgeois society. Rather, he realized that it is not enough for the capitalist to have a social structure that allows profits to be maximized; the social system must also be able to continuously reproduce the conditions under which the capitalists can exist at all. The economic and the non-economic spheres of society, Marx concluded, exist together in a dialectical interrelationship, with each producing and influencing the other.

Marx thus saw reality as a vast intermingling web of relations, each influencing the others and each in turn being influenced by the others. To attempt to study this complicated web, however, poses an awkward problem — it is impossible to tell just where one element ends and another begins, since each is an interpenetrating part of the other. As Marxist scholar Bertell Ollman points out, "What emerges from this interpretation is that the problem Marx faces in his exposition is not how to link separate parts, but how to individuate instrumental units in a social whole which finds expression everywhere."

For this reason, Marx's writings are often imprecise and ambiguous, not because he was unsure about what he wanted to say, but because there is no verbal manner in which to say it precisely. As a result, one writer has noted, Marx's words are somewhat like bats; one can see in them something of a mouse and something of a bird.

Marxian definitions and concepts thus mean different things when they are used to examine different aspects of any given social relationship. The Marxian concept of "mode of production", for instance, is at various times and places defined as "civil society", "the ensemble of social relationships", "the economic structure of society", "the economic foundation", "the sum of productive forces, capital funds, and social forms of intercourse", and "social existence". Since the meanings of these words varied according to the specific relationship under study, Engels points out, there are no "fixed, cut-to-measure, once and for all applicable definitions which things must be made to fit". "We are dealing here with definite functions which must be expressed in definite categories."

In order to rationally examine this interpenetrating social whole, it is necessary to intellectually divide that reality into sub-units. The particular manner in which Marx chose to divide society into components centered around the economic system, and led to the Marxian emphasis on the dynamics of class interactions within economic structures.

This is not, however, the only valid way of dividing society into parts in order to understand it. Since all of these intellectual divisions and categories are artificial, we are free to "carve up" capitalist society in any way we wish, in order to more closely examine any particular part of it. In examining capitalism's economic structures, Marx divided society into the classes "workers" and "owners". If we wish to examine the gender constructions of capitalist society, however, we must divide society into the categories of "male" and "female". If racial or national relationships are our interest, we must divide society into the various racial and national groups and examine their interrelationship. Since reality is a seamless interpenetrating whole, it makes no difference how we divide it up into intellectual categories, so long as we recognize that all of our divisions are arbitrary and artificial—none is any more or less valid than the others.

The descriptions Marx gives for this simultaneously-interpenetrating social process are, however, difficult for many to understand in a society such as ours, which views things linearly in a one-to-one cause and effect relationship. Therefore, after Marx's death, those Marxists who were unable to grasp the implications of the Marxian concept of relational totality took it upon themselves to modify, simplify and re-define Marxism. This new conception was "dialectical materialism", and was adopted by the Leninists.

These socialists reduced all of Marx's profound insights to the simple formula, "Economic conditions determine consciousness". In other words, these theorists concluded, prevailing economic conditions directly determined all of society's relationships, including such non-economic spheres as the family, the state, religion, morality and law.

Marx, however, had concluded that the relationship between the economic and non-economic spheres is relational and dialectical, not a linear cause-and-effect relationship. The economic sphere cannot "cause" or "determine" the non-economic superstructure, since the organization of this superstructure plays a large role in determining the structure of economic relationships. The economic determinists, for example, assert that legal property regulations are a mere "reflection" of existing capitalist economic relationships, but they ignore the fact that legal property laws are themselves a major determining factor in the structure of economic relationships. Non-economic structures are in fact an integral part of the economic relationships which they supposedly "reflect". "Productive forces and social relations," Marx writes, "[are] different sides of the development of the social individual":

> In the actual world, civil law, morality, the family, civil society, the state, etc., remain in existence, only they have become moments— states of existence and being of humans—which have no validity in isolation, but dissolve and engender one another.

This conception of history depends on our ability to expound the real process of production, starting out from the material production of life itself, and to comprehend the form of intercourse connected with this and created by this mode of production (i.e., civil society in its various stages), as the basis of all history, and to show it in its actions as state; to explain all the different theoretical products and forms of consciousness, religion, philosophy, ethics, etc., etc., and trace their origins and growth from that basis; by which means, of course, the whole thing can be depicted in its totality (and therefore, too, the reciprocal action of these various sides on one another).

Engels says, "Political, judicial, philosophical, religious, literary, artistic, etc., development is based on economic development, but all these react upon one another and also upon the economic base."

Although Marx never asserted that human social reality was based upon narrow economic structures, he and Engels deserve much of the blame for fueling this interpretation. Although he on occasion refers to his outlook as "naturalistic materialism" and "consistent naturalism or humanism ... distinct from both idealism and materialism", for the most part Marx continued to call himself a "materialist" to separate himself clearly from Hegelian idealism, and thus reinforced later deterministic interpretations of his outlook.

Marx also continued to deliberately overemphasize the role of economic structures in all of his works, since he was responding to idealist German philosophers who tended to give economic relationships no role at all in human affairs. In his *1844 Economic and Philosophic Manuscripts*, Marx explicitly points out, "For this reason, it will be found that the interconnection between political economy and the state, law, ethics, civil life, etc., is touched upon in the present work only to the extent to which political economy itself expressly touches upon those subjects."

Nevertheless, both Marx and Engels attacked those who reduced Marxism to simple economic determinism. Engels wrote, "According to the materialist conception of history, the determining moment in history is ultimately the production and reproduction of real life. More than this neither Marx nor I have ever asserted. If therefore somebody twists this into the statement that the economic moment is the only determining one, he transforms it into a meaningless, abstract and absurd phrase."

Marx never lost sight of the interpenetration and co-determination of the economic and non-economic spheres. Towards the end of his life, he intended to write a whole series of books detailing the structure of the total capitalist mode of production, and intended to examine the roles of various non-economic relationships in the reproduction of capitalist society. "The wealth and diversity of the subjects to be treated," he wrote, "could have been compressed into one work only in a purely aphoristic style; while an aphoristic presentation of this kind, for its part, would have given the impression of arbitrary systematism. I shall therefore publish the critique of law, ethics, politics, etc., in a series of distinct, independent pamphlets, and afterwards try in a special work to present them again as an interconnected whole, showing the interrelationships of the separate parts."

Unfortunately, Marx did not live long enough to finish his projected series. He completed a work on capitalist economics, *Capital*, but was never able to begin his works on the other spheres of capitalist society. Similarly, Marx was unable to begin any works on the various non-economic relationships of oppression in bourgeois society — sexism, racism, heterosexism, nationalism — and how these relationships influenced and were influenced by the economic class structures of capitalism.

Although Marx often referred to "laws of the dialectic" and "laws of capitalist motion", it is apparent that these took on, in the Marxian conception, a definition which is very different from those given to them by the Leninists and other "scientific Marxists". Marx, as we have seen, viewed the development of the capitalist social system as being the result of the mutual interactions of many various elements, and found it impossible to explain how capitalism (or any other human society) works unless each of these elements were described and understood.

But, Marx realized, what these elements *are* is at the same time dependent upon what they *were*. Therefore, it is also necessary to understand how these various elements developed as they did, through their mutual interactions, and how this process of development affects the possible directions they can take in the future. The chances of future development in any particular direction, therefore, are limited by the developmental process which these elements have already undergone. In other words, what *will be* is dependent to a large extent upon what *has already been*.

Marx referred to this dialectical limit as a "law of motion". This "law", he pointed out, was not a predetermined necessity, but rather a tendency—"Law is chance". Engels writes that it was never their intention to say that the human social development which they described was "inevitable" or "predetermined":

> Marx does not dream of attempting to prove by this that the process was historically necessary. On the contrary, after he has proven from history that in fact the process has already partially occurred, and partially must occur in the future, he then also characterizes it as a process which develops in accordance with a definite dialectical law. That is all.

Thus, Marx's "laws" were not intended to be deterministic predictions; they were merely tendencies which result from the development of human society through co-determining entities. The dialectic is a way of looking at the process of social change after it has already begun, not a predictive method of determining the future development of human society. As Marx points out, the process of social change is undertaken by the actions of free living humans, who can at any time drastically alter the direction of those tendencies:

> Reality is only a product of the preceding intercourse of individuals themselves. Thus the Communists in practice treat the conditions created up to now by production and intercourse as inorganic conditions, without, however, imagining that it was the plan

or the destiny of previous individuals to give them that material, and without believing that these conditions were inorganic for the individuals creating them.

Marx pointed out that "history" and "natural laws" are simply abstractions from actual human practice; history is produced by the actions of living humans, not the other way around. "People make their own history," Marx wrote. "History is nothing other than people engaged in social practice":

> History does nothing; it "possesses no wealth", it "wages no battles". It is people, real people, that do all that, that possess and fight; "history" is not a person apart, using humans as a means for its own particular aims; history is nothing other than the activity of humans pursuing their aims.

Those who assert that humans actions are "determined" by "economic laws" have merely substituted one alienation for another. The dialectical materialists, having rejected the postulate that God or ideas are the moving forces of human reality, instead assert that "natural laws" and "economics" are, and have simply substituted the abstraction of "economic law" for that of "divine law". The economic determinists, like the religious idealists, deny the role of human actions in history.

Marx rejected this notion, and asserted that humans, acting within the limits imposed upon them by their circumstances, produced their own surroundings. None of it was "predetermined" or "inevitable", and none of it was produced by any "laws". The process of scientifically understanding something, Engels writes, does not involve formulating a set of deterministic laws about it, but rather to "allocate to each its place in the interconnections of nature", and to understand this dialectical interconnection.

Thus, it is completely foreign to Marx's viewpoint to assert that the economic struggle is the "cause" of social development, or that the conflict between economic classes is the source of all other social conflicts. Rather, Marx asserted, all of these elements are dialectical, interpenetrating and co-determining, and must be understood as parts of a totality if they are to be understood at all.

Engels writes:

> So long as we consider things as static and lifeless, each one by itself, alongside of and after each other, it is true that we do not run up against any contradictions in them. . . But the position is quite different as soon as we consider things in their motion, their change, their life, their reciprocal influence on one another. Then we immediately become involved in contradictions.

The proletarian revolution, Marx concludes, is dependent upon several historical and social trends, but its driving force is much more basic. The masses of working people are, he says, in the final analysis driven to revolt because of the debilitating conditions of a fragmented social life, because of the "contradiction between its humanity and its situation, which is an open, clear and absolute negation of its humanity."

To rectify the situation and remove the artificial restraints imposed by capitalist social institutions, radical changes must be made. However, Marx notes, "To be radical is to grasp things by the root. But for humans, the root is humans themselves." Marx declares, "The criticism of religion ends with the doctrine that Humanity is the highest being for humans."

Thus, Marx concludes, the essence of human activity is to change their social relationships through praxis, through conscious effort. "The philosophers have only interpreted the world in various ways," he says. "The point is to change it."

Marx realized that revolutionary change was not automatic or self-fulfilling, and was not produced through the actions of impersonal "economic laws". If revolutionary change were to take place, it could only be accomplished by human beings who have examined the existing social structure and have determined the interactions and relationships which define and form it. Engels writes:

When we consider and reflect upon Nature at large or the history of humans or our own intellectual activity, at first we see the picture of an endless entanglement of relations and reactions, permutations and combinations, in which nothing remains what, where and as it is, but everything moves, changes, comes into being and passes away. We see, therefore, at first the picture as a whole, with its individual parts still more or less kept into the background; we observe the movements, transitions, and connections, rather than the things which move, combine and connect.

This conception, correctly as it expresses the general character of the picture of appearances as a whole, does not suffice to explain the details which make up this picture, and so long as we do not understand these, we do not have a clear idea of the whole picture.

Engels continues:

In order to understand these details, we must detach them from their natural and historical connections and examine each one separately, its nature, special causes, effects, etc. This is, primarily, the task of natural science and historical research.

But this method of work has left us as a legacy the habit of observing natural objects and processes in isolation, apart from their connection with the vast whole; of observing them in repose, not as variables; in their death, not their life.

Further, Engels adds:

We find upon closer examination that the two poles of thesis and anti-thesis, positive and negative, e.g., are as inseparable as they are opposed, and that despite all of their opposition they mutually interpenetrate. And we find, in like manner, that cause and effect are only conceptions which hold good in their application to individual cases; but as soon as we consider the individual cases in their general connection to the universe as a whole, they run into each other; and they become confounded when we contemplate that general action and reaction in which cause and effect are eternally changing places, so that what is effect here and now will be cause there and then, and vice versa.

Engels concludes:

> An exact representation of the universe, its evolution, the development of humans, and the reflection of this evolution in the minds of people, can therefore only be obtained by the methods of dialectics, with its constant regard to the innumerable actions and reactions of life and death, or progressive and regressive changes.

To understand the totality of bourgeois society, then, we must understand it in all its forms and facets. We must move beyond the simple economic sphere of class relationships, and understand the other social divisions and relationships which make up capitalist society. The source of the capitalist class's power is not merely that it controls capital and thus places workers in a disadvantaged economic position. The ruling class's power comes from the fact that it is able to implement and reproduce a set of interconnecting social relationships which safeguard its position of privilege, and that it is able to defend these relationships from the attempts of the oppressed to change them.

We must therefore systematically examine each of these social relationships as they exist in modern bourgeois society. And, once we have seen how they support and protect each other, we must determine the best way to undermine each of them and replace them.

Feminism

Feminism can best be described as the study of the relationships through which women are subordinated to men, for the purpose of changing these relationships. It is not enough to understand or interpret these relationships, feminists assert—the point is to change them.

Most feminists refer to the system of male domination over female as "patriarchy". "Patriarchy," writes Adrienne Rich, "is the power of the fathers, a familial, social, ideological, political system in which men—by force, direct pressure, or through ritual, tradition, law and language, customs, etiquette, education and division of labor—determine what part women shall or shall not play, and in which the female is everywhere subsumed under the male."

Patriarchical relationships abound in modern society. Throughout history, the laws which pertain to women in such matters as marriage, divorce and rape have been essentially property laws, treating women as if they were the property of men. Marriage can be considered as a property relationship in which men agree to provide the economic means of life to women in exchange for exclusive sexual rights. Rape, rather than being considered a crime against a woman, has historically been more often viewed as an offense against the husband or father whose "property" has thus been damaged. At the same time, laws and customs concerning sexual practices consist for the most part of control over *female* sexual practices, not male.

Gender roles have long been used to exploit women economically. The social roles of "wife" and "husband" determine that women get "female" jobs, such as nurses, teachers or secretaries, while men retain the positions of economic power and influence. Whenever they do manage to enter a traditionally "male" occupation, women are paid less than men and are kept in the lower rungs of the job ladder. Sexual harassment on the job also serves to remind women of their place in the social hierarchy; sexual harassment is a control issue, not a sex issue—it uses sexism to keep women in a subordinate role.

The structure of the nuclear family also acts to protect patriarchical interests. The traditional family (a husband, a wife and their offspring) locks women into "housekeeping" and "child-rearing" roles, thus limiting their social and economic power and leaving the men free to enter the "real world".

Other social relationships also reflect the impact of patriarchical gender roles. The educational system, through which children are acculturated and indoctrinated, sets out rigid gender roles which cannot be violated. Boys are expected to take shop classes or college preparatory courses, so they can get jobs in business, trades or industry. Girls are expected to take home economics, typing and secretarial courses, which prepare them for their "careers" at home or in low-wage, dead-end jobs.

The advertising industry launches a constant barrage of patriarchical messages at men and women alike. Sexual stereotypes and idealized "sex symbols" are used to sell everything from soap to automobiles. The post-World War II economic boom succeeded in large part because the advertising industry was able to subtly manipulate the woman's expected role as "wife" and "mother" to keep consumer demand high and thus find an outlet for the huge numbers of commodities being turned out in American factories.

And, if some women began to question all of these social roles and stereotypes, the Freudian psychologists were there to speak knowingly of "penis envy", and thus to provide a "scientific" justification for women to "keep their place" and not "try to be a man".

"So deeply embedded is patriarchy," writes Kate Millett, "that the character structure it creates in both sexes is perhaps even more a habit of mind and a way of life than a political system."

It is the goal of feminism to break this "way of life", and to end the patriarchical domination of females by males. As Hester Eisenstein writes, "At the heart of feminism is an egalitarian impulse, seeking to free women from oppression by removing all of the obstacles to their political, economic and sexual self-determination."

This goal of a non-oppressive, egalitarian society is shared by the socialists as well. It is, therefore, no surprise that socialists and feminists have had much to say to each other.

Marx and Engels wrote at some length of gender and familial roles within capitalist society. In his work *Origin of the Family, Private Property and the State*, Engels set out what would become the "classic" exposition of the Marxian view on "the woman question". "The first class opposition that appears in history," Engels writes, "coincides with the development of the antagonism between man and woman in monogamous marriage, and the first class oppression coincides with that of the female sex by the male."

Engels based much of his sociological work on the research of Lewis Henry Morgan, an American anthropologist who did field work among the Iroquois tribes in New York. Morgan mistakenly believed that, in the past, virtually all human societies had been matriarchical — that is, that women held the dominant social positions. Today, we know that there is very little evidence to support this view. But Engels, following Morgan, concluded that the relations between male and female had been egalitarian until the appearance of private property:

> Monogamy arose from the concentration of considerable wealth in the hands of a single individual — a man — and from the need to bequeath this wealth to the children of that man and no other. For this purpose, the monogamy of the woman was required, not that of the man; so this monogamy of the woman did not in any way interfere with open or concealed polygamy on the part of the man.

This need to control the reproductive activities of women in order to insure that one's heirs were truly one's biological offspring, Engels concludes, forms the basis for the nuclear family. "The modern family," Engels writes, "is founded on the open or disguised domestic slavery of women." In the *Communist Manifesto*, Marx writes, "On what foundation is the present family, the bourgeois family, based? On capital, on private gain."

However, Marx and Engels thought they could see an approaching end to this domestic slavery. Since the family existed only to bequeath property and wealth, and since only the capitalists had any wealth to bequeath, Marx concluded that "In its completely developed form, this family exists only among the bourgeoisie." Among the working class the situation was different. "Here," Engels writes, "there is no property, for the preservation and inheritance of which monogamy and male supremacy was established; hence, there is no incentive to make this male supremacy effective." In other words, Marx and Engels declared, as soon as private property was abolished, patriarchy would fall by itself.

In the writings which he was able to finish before his death, Marx tended to look at all of capitalist society in strictly economic terms. Since he also assumed that gender relationships were the product of property relationships, it is not surprising that most of his comments concerning women were made from an economic point of view.

Women, Marx pointed out, were "doubly exploited". Not only were they subjected to horrible conditions of exploitation in the industrial factories (where they worked twelve-hour days for pitiful wages), but they were also forced to perform many hours of work in the home, for which they were not paid at all.

Marx also noted that female workers made up a large portion of the "reserve army of the unemployed". In the Marxist economic schema, the wages of workers rose or fell as the supply of those workers fluctuated against demand. If economic expansion required more workers than were readily available, wages rose as employers were forced to bid against each other for scarce workers. If the supply of laborers exceeded demand, however, wages fell as employers were able to give jobs to workers who were willing to work for less.

It was, Marx pointed out, advantageous for employers to have a large number of people who were more or less permanently unemployed, the "reserve army". In this way, business owners had a constant oversupply of laborers and were thus able to keep wages down and profits up. In late 19th century Europe and the US, most of this reserve army was made up of women and children who were compelled to work for lower wages, and who thus enabled businesses to keep profits as high as possible.

Marx's analysis of the role of women in bourgeois society was, we can now see, shallow and incomplete. Even within his chosen emphasis on economic factors, Marx failed to examine the effects of gender roles. He points out on several occasions that women were economically disadvantaged, noting, "The large workshops prefer to buy the labor of women and children, because this costs less than that of a man," but he ignored the social factors which produced and propagated this disparity between the genders. Instead of examining the effects of patriarchical roles on bourgeois economic and family structures, Marx abstracted these away, and utilized economic categories which deliberately ignored the effects of patriarchy:

The value of labor power is determined by the necessaries of life habitually required by the average laborer. The quantity of these necessities is known in any given epoch of a given society, and can therefore be treated as a constant magnitude. What changes is the value of these quantities. There are, besides, two factors which enter into the determination of the value of labor power. One, the expenses of developing this power, which expenses vary with the mode of production; and the other, its natural diversity, the difference between the labor power of men and women, of children and adults. The employment of these different sorts of labor power, an employment which is, in turn, made necessary by the mode of production, makes a great difference in the cost of maintaining the family of the laborer, and in the value of the labor of the adult male. Both these factors, however, are excluded from the following investigation.

Thus, while Marx recognized that there were major differences in the economic and social standing of women and men, in his economic analysis he abstracts from these differences and treats all workers as an undifferentiated mass, as if they were all "adult males".

Ironically, employers and business owners have not failed to make this distinction. One of the most common justifications used by employers who pay their female workers less than the males is that "men need to support their family with their wages, while the women don't".

Marx also abstracted away from any discussion of the roles played by men and women within the family, and how these family structures affected the socio-economic order:

The laborer consumes in a two-fold way. While producing, he consumes by his labor the means of production, and converts them into products with higher value than that of the capital which bought it. On the other hand, the laborer turns the money paid to him for his labor power into means of subsistence; this is his individual consumption. The laborer's productive consumption and his individual consumption are thus totally distinct. In the former, he acts as the motive power of capital and belongs to the capitalist. In the latter, he belongs to himself, and performs his necessary vital function outside the process of production.

When treating the working day, we saw that the laborer is often compelled to make his individual consumption a mere incident of production. In such a case, he supplies himself with the necessaries of life in order to maintain his labor power, just as coal and water are supplies to the steam engine and oil to the wheel. His means of consumption, in that case, are the mere means of consumption required by a means of production; his individual consumption is directly productive consumption. This, however, appears to be an abuse not essentially pertaining to capitalist production.

The process of maintaining individual and productive consumption, i.e., of keeping laborers alive and producing new laborers, is performed by the social institution of the family. Marx, as we have seen, failed to analyze the role of the family within capitalist production, judging it to be "not essential".

To feminists, however, the study of family roles and gender divisions within the family are absolutely critical. As Batya Weinbaum points out, "The 'laborer' does not supply himself with necessaries in order to maintain his own labor power. More often, 'he' gets a wife to do so for him. Hence the structural difficulty of surviving either as an unmarried or woman worker."

Capitalists, just as Marx, tend to ignore the vital economic role played by the nuclear family. Unlike the slaveholder, who had to be personally responsible for seeing that his laborers received the food, clothing and shelter they needed, the capitalist business owner simply expects that his laborers' needs will be provided by the family structure, and that the employer will not have to bother himself with such a responsibility.

This social structure thus molds the attitude of capitalist society to the gender roles carried out by women within the family. When a woman cooks, cleans and keeps house for her family, capitalism ignores it or treats it as a social "given". If this same woman, however, cooks, cleans and keeps house for her neighbor for a salary, capitalism treats this activity as "production", and capitalist bosses derive profit from this production. As Weinbaum puts it, "Household relations modify production relations, as well as the other way around."

Feminists have long pointed out that family relationships have a vital effect on economic structures. In early non-capitalist societies, the extended family unit was made up of individuals who pooled their labor to provide for the family's collective needs. Husband, wife, children and relatives all worked in the fields and performed other chores in order to produce food, clothing and other necessities. In this situation, the necessities of life are collectively produced by the family members, and the economic position of each member of the family is roughly equal to that of the others (although the overall social position of women is very different).

In capitalism, however, commodities are purchased rather than produced, and therefore, within the family unit, wages are pooled rather than labor. As a result, production is collectivized outside the family, in the factory, rather than inside the family, as in the family-worked agrarian plot. The family members in capitalist society thus become analogous to workers who bring wealth to the head of the household; this "head of the family" dispenses these resources as he sees fit. And, because of gender structures, the head of this household is almost invariably male.

This further undermines the Marxian assumption that a laborer's production and consumption is an individual activity. Marx assumed that the basis for capitalism lay in the fact that the means of production, capital, were owned by a small portion of the population, and that the large mass of people, with no means of production of their own, were forced to sell their labor power to the capitalists to make a living. Now, however, we can see that, because of patriarchical gender relationships, the male head of the household not only sells his own labor power, but also that of his wife and daughters, and that he retains control over the wages earned by the rest of his family.

Marx never examined the patriarchical components within the capitalist family, and abstracted from gender differences in all of his economic analyses. Had Marx lived to investigate the role of patriarchy in maintaining bourgeois society as thoroughly as he did the economics of capitalism, his conclusions may have been quite different.

It therefore fell to feminism to accomplish the analysis of gender roles in social and familial structures. Feminists have pointed out that the family unit is vital in instilling patriarchical ideas of authority and gender roles, in men and women alike. As Shulamith Firestone points out, "This then is the oppressive climate in which the normal child grows up. From the beginning, he is sensitive to the hierarchy of power. He knows that in every way, physically, emotionally, economically, he is completely dependent on, thus at the mercy of, his two parents, whoever they may be." And, the child further learns, within the relationship of husband and wife, the male is everywhere superior.

Firestone views the basis of the family in capitalist society as essentially sexual and economic — a husband pays wages, in the form of the economic necessities of life, to a wife in exchange for sex and housework. Even if the woman has a job of her own and can support herself economically, Firestone points out, when she has a child and must leave work, she again becomes economically dependent on her husband.

The only way to end patriarchy, Firestone concludes, is to end the family structure which produces and propagates it. "To make both women and children totally independent," she writes, "would be to eliminate not just the patriarchical nuclear family, but the biological family itself."

Because Marx never examined the role of gender relationships in bourgeois society, he tended to view "the woman question" as a subspecies of "the worker question", and simply assumed that, once capitalism was abolished, the liberation of women would follow. The emancipation of women, Marx concluded, would result from the integration of women into the workplace and their subsequent organization alongside male workers to fight the class enemy. As Engels puts it:

> With the transformation of the means of production into social property, there will disappear also wage labor, the proletariat, and

therefore the necessity for a certain statistically calculable number of women to surrender themselves for money.

> This will be answered when a new generation has grown up; a generation of men who have never in their lives known what it is to buy a woman's surrender with money or with any other social instrument of power; a generation of women who have never known what it is to give themselves to a man from any other consideration than real love, or to refuse to give themselves to their lover from fear of the economic consequences. When these people are in the world, they will care precious little what anybody today thinks they ought to do; they will make their own practice and their corresponding public opinion about the practice of each individual — and that will be the end of it.

Marx's assertion that the worker's struggle will automatically lead to the liberation of women has been attacked by feminists ever since, and has been a cause of feminist hostility to Marxism and socialism. "Marx and Engels," notes Robin Morgan, "didn't deal with half the human species." Few radical women are willing to participate in a social movement that considers their situation to be secondary or less important. Myra Tanner Weiss describes this attitude, "First, we would win socialism. Then, women would get their emancipation. Implicit in this notion is the conclusion that, meanwhile, the women should shut up! Don't divide the working class!"

Marx's implicit conclusion was made brutally explicit by Lenin. In a letter to radical feminist Clara Zetkin, Lenin heaped criticism upon her practice of holding meetings to discuss the liberation of women from male domination. "I have been told," Lenin wrote, "that at the meetings arranged for reading and discussion with working women, sex and marriage problems come first. They are said to be the main objects of interest in your political instruction and educational work. I could not believe my ears when I heard that!" Apparently, Lenin could not believe that women would prefer to talk about women's concerns over (mostly male) workers' concerns.

Since then, Leninists have consistently dismissed feminism as "revisionist" and a "bourgeois deviation". While they try to work with women on "workplace issues", such as equal pay and sexual harassment, other feminist concerns get only lip service from the Leninists. Such issues only divide the working class, they say, and delay the coming of the socialist revolution which will liberate women. As Evelyn Reed, of the Socialist Workers Party, announced (apparently seriously), "Since the interests of the Party are paramount . . . the primary duty of women and Negro leaders is first of all to be Marxists, and only after that women and Negroes." Activist Alan Woods wrote, "In order to bring about the socialist revolution, it is necessary to unite the working class and its organisations, cutting across all lines of language, nationality, race, religion and sex. This implies, on the one hand, that the working class must take upon itself the task of fighting against all forms of oppression and exploitation, and place itself at the head of all the oppressed layers of society, and on the other, must decisively reject all attempts to divide it—even when these attempts are made by sections of the oppressed themselves."

When socialists have admitted the necessity for feminist actions, they have most often, like Lenin, attempted to run these movements themselves, for their own ends. Most female radicals are relegated to what may be called the "Ladies' Auxiliary of the Left", and play at best a minor role within the larger organization. As Shulamith Firestone points out, most Leninists use feminist issues as "no more than a useful 'radicalizing' tool to recruit women into the 'larger struggle' ".

One of the largest Leninist groups in the United States today, the Revolutionary Communist Party, says little about feminist revolution, but says a lot about the role feminists can play in the socialist revolution. "Women in the working class," the RCP announces, "will play a crucial role, and the fight against the oppression of women will be a powerful force for the working class as a whole, in the proletarian revolution in the US." The RCP points with pride to the growing number of women in its ranks, and declares, "All this strengthens the basis both for the fight against the oppression of woman and for women to play a powerful role in the overall class struggle." The RCP, like Lenin, asserts that "women's issues" are unimportant by themselves; they are useful simply because they draw women into the "real fight" — the economic class struggle.

Needless to say, feminist radicals have come to view the Leninist solution to patriarchical relationships as a non-solution. Batya Weinbaum satirically notes, "We find it easier and more comforting to put off the 'woman question' in the hope that, though sexism might be bad now, after the revolution, somehow, it all gets better. . . This 'after the revolution' trust has been eulogized, much as the belief in the next world or the afterlife seems to operate for those with more traditional religious convictions."

On the whole, moreover, Leninist and socialist practice has not been much more sympathetic to feminist concerns than its theory. During its 1950's debate over the relationship between feminism and socialism, the Socialist Workers Party refused to allow women the right to caucus within the party, saying that a woman's first loyalty should be to the "working class struggle".

Other Leninist parties have paid lip service to ending sexism, but have continued to stack their decision-making bodies with men and a few token women, a practice followed by ruling parties in the USSR and elsewhere. "In conceding a few powerful positions to a small number of exceptional women," Hester Eisenstein complained, "present arrangements of access to power, privilege and decision-making will remain overwhelmingly in the hands of those who now rule."

In the 1960's, the "New Left", a loose amalgamation of student groups, labor militants and anarchists, proved itself to be no more sympathetic to the fight against sexism than had the "Old Left". In 1964, Stokely Carmichael of the Student National Coordinating Committee refused to accept a position paper discussing the role of women in the Movement. "The only position for women in SNCC," he declared, "is prone." Others of the New Left derided the feminist movement as "pussy power". In the Students for a Democratic Society, one feminist remarked, women "made peanut butter, waited on tables, cleaned up, got laid. That was their role."

In Britain, the Women's Liberation Workshop declared in disgust, "The support of the male radical is always conditional. As long as you dedicate yourself to his political causes and accept his buck-passing analysis of your oppression (it's capitalism, not me, sweetheart) you will be given some time off and occasionally — when politically expedient — some patronizing interest." In 1969, feminist writer Marge Piercy bluntly asked, "The Movement is supposed to be for human liberation; how come the condition inside of it is no better than on the outside?"

Leninists and socialists responded to these feminist criticisms with vague references to "inherited consciousness" or to the "effects of alienation" or to ideology "lagging behind" the changing economic conditions. In the aftermath of the revolutions in Russia, China, Cuba and elsewhere, however, it became clear that the Leninist contention that sexism would disappear after the revolution was at best wishful thinking and at worst a deliberate fraud.

In those Leninist nations which had overthrown capitalism and instituted state control over the means of production, the social roles of women remained virtually unchanged. The USSR, in the early 1920's, experimented widely and boldly with the elimination of old gender roles, and made large strides towards eradicating sexism and patriarchical structures. However, economic and political realities soon forced the Bolsheviks to reverse this trend. To survive, the Soviet Union had to begin a massive program of industrial expansion, and this necessitated a social order of strict centralization and regimentation. Everything in the Soviet Union was tied to the single goal of increasing industrial output through the Five Year Plans.

Originally, the USSR had decided that, unless women's household work could be collectivized, Soviet women could never be freed from household and family roles, and thus would never be able to participate fully in a communal society. Thus, the Soviet Government launched a massive campaign to provide communal facilities such as day care centers and central laundries, providing a central pool to do these things and freeing the majority of women from these tasks.

Under the pressing weight of the industrialization program, however, the attempt to free women from household tasks was redirected. Now, women were to be freed from household tasks not so they could participate freely in communal society, but simply so they could be moved out of the house and into the factories. To further increase the number of hands available for the industrialization program, the Leninists passed laws which outlawed abortions and made divorces more difficult to obtain. A propaganda blitz was begun to convince Soviet women to have as many children as possible.

In China, Chairman Mao's ruling bureaucracy outlawed such crude sexist relics as the binding of women's feet, female infanticide and "arranged" marriages. However, women continued to be politically and socially subservient to men. After feminist complaints that the Communist Party leadership contained only a handful of women (including Chairman Mao's wife), the Maoist ideologues answered with murmurs about "the difficulty of uprooting relics of class society". This prompted American feminist Susan Brownmiller to retort, "It seems to me that a country that wiped out the tse-tse fly can, by fiat, put an equal number of women on the Central Committee."

In Nicaragua, the bastion of Latin machismo, the Sandinistas responded to feminist concerns with a half-hearted campaign to talk husbands into doing their share of the housework. The Nicaraguan Women's Association (AMNLAE) was single-minded in its support of the (mostly male) Sandinista elite, and didn't even murmur in complaint when the FSLN refused to make abortions legal.

On the whole, radical feminists have not been very impressed with the track record of the "socialist" countries. Juliet Mitchell points out that, while the liberation of women was expanded in some areas (the Leninists made real gains in expanding educational opportunities for women), the Communist countries have failed to bring about "authentic liberation". Others were not so charitable. Adrienne Rich writes that Marxism is "the 'revolution' of a wheel which returns in the end to the same place; the 'revolving door' of a politics which has 'liberated' women only to use them, and only within the limits of male tolerance."

Shulamith Firestone has been the sharpest feminist critic of Marxism and socialism. Of Marx and Engels, she bluntly declares, "About the condition of women as an oppressed class they knew next to nothing, recognizing it only where it overlaps with economics." Firestone jettisoned the Marxian economic dialectic for a sexual one, which she called "the materialist view of history based on sex itself."

In this view, every aspect of modern society can be looked at as a result of the patriarchical position of men over women. "Sexism," as Robin Morgan declares, "is the root oppression, the one which, until and unless we uproot it, will continue to put forth the branches of racism, class hatred, ageism, competition, ecological disaster, and economic exploitation." According to these radical feminists, the struggle against patriarchy is the "real" struggle, and all other social movements are merely subspecies of the feminist revolution. Socialists, of course, see the class struggle as the "real" fight. The debate over this proposition has not ceased to rage.

One school of thought, the "socialist-feminists", attempted to find a middle ground between these two outlooks. The socialist-feminists accept the various feminist criticisms of Marxism, but also assert that feminist struggles must be viewed in their social and economic context. It is true, they say, that capitalism makes use of gender roles to serve economic ends, but it is also true that sexism predates capitalism by a considerable length of time; capitalist economic inequalities can therefore be viewed as merely the latest method used by males to keep females in a subordinate social position.

As Hester Eisenstein, one of the earliest socialist-feminists, says:

Ought one to castigate feminism because it is insufficiently revolutionary and geared to the concerns of the working class? Or ought one to take a longer view and ask, what would become of present social arrangements, in the capitalist West and indeed in most societies, capitalist and communist, if all of the demands of the women's movement were met with respect to all women?

A feminist analysis that failed to take account of the effects of class, and of the impact of the needs of a late monopoly capitalist economy on the position of women domestically and internationally, would be less than adequate as a tool either of analysis or prediction.

The early women's rights movements in Europe and the United States were, for the most part, led by the wives and daughters of the educated and wealthy elite. These feminists did not question the structures or assumptions of bourgeois society — they simply wanted to play a larger role within it.

As a result, the early "suffragettes" saw no connection between their programs and those of other radical social movements. "The great distinctive advantage possessed by the workingmen of this republic," said Susan B. Anthony, "is that the son of the humblest citizen, black or white, has equal chances with the son of the richest in the land." Anthony was referring to the right to vote, which, she incorrectly assumed, gave all men equal power. Anthony never considered that Blacks did not have equal voting power until 1964, and that poor working class men have very little political or economic power compared to the wealthy captains of industry.

Because most early feminists were white, well-educated and wealthy, they tended to view all social relationships from this viewpoint. As a result, they tended to generalize their viewpoint to "all women", and thus ignored the very real differences in the social circumstances of black women and white, or wealthy women and poor.

Many feminists, being from wealthy families, dismissed the labor movement and the struggles of working people. Susan B. Anthony went so far as to encourage educated women to take jobs as strikebreakers and scabs if it helped them to enter male-dominated trades. (It did not help that, at the time, nearly all labor unions disqualified women from membership.) Many suffragettes called for property qualifications for voting, which would have allowed wealthy women to vote but not poor working class men. Such feminists were unable to see the social divisions between poor women and rich, since such an analysis would have undermined their own privileged social position. Instead, they were compelled to limit their fight to "equal participation" in existing society.

And, because most early feminists were white, they tended towards indifference or open hostility towards the civil rights movement and the fight for African-American liberation. During the women's suffrage marches in the 1910's, Black women were instructed to march in separate blocks in order to avoid offending the sensibilities of Southern white women. An argument used by a number of suffragettes was that giving "educated" (i.e., white) women the right to vote would "counterbalance" the "ignorant Negroes".

Today, such open hostility has disappeared, but many feminists continue to cut themselves off from the other progressive movements. Many mainstream feminist groups, such as the National Organization for Women, limit their social reforms to obtaining "equal access" and "equal opportunity" for women, without calling into question the social institutions within which women are to gain equal roles. It is difficult to understand how the act of allowing a woman to become a corporate manager, a government bureaucrat or a military general as easily as a man would be an improvement on the existing social situation.

Because, even today, most feminists are white, they have tended to equate the social struggles of women with the social struggles of African-Americans or Latinos, and thus fail to acknowledge that many women *are* African-American or Latina, and that racism has as much an impact on their lives as sexism. One Black feminist, tired of hearing constant references to the "struggles of Blacks and women", shot back sarcastically, "Ain't I a woman?"

Several radical feminists have issued a call to establish a "women's culture", in which all women must band together to fight for their mutual interests. This cult of "womanhood", however, ignores the profound differences between women of different cultures and different socio-economic classes, and tends to place all women in the same social position. The needs and outlooks of a Black woman in Nigeria, however, are not the same as those of a white woman attorney in Manhattan. Similarly, a female worker in a Ford motor company assembly line has more social, political and economic interests in common with the male worker on the line next to her than she does with Donald Trump's wife. Essentially, the "women's culture" of these feminist "universalists" is nothing more than a variant of the white Anglo-European culture within which they have lived, and which they are projecting onto everybody else.

The "universalist" movement within feminism seems, however, to be fading out, and is in the process of being replaced by a more flowing and multi-polar view of industrial society. "There is a growing understanding," writes Ann Snitow, "that the recognition of gender as a significant political category in no way bypasses the crucial differences among women; of class, race and sexual preference."

With this understanding has come a greater awareness of the interconnections between feminism and socialism. It is now possible to recognize that the feminists and the socialists have approached a common problem — how to build an egalitarian society — from two different but complementary points of view. The two outlooks, as we have seen, have much to say to each other. Both Marxism and feminism have, in the past, tended to view themselves as the primary social justice movement, with all others being secondary to it. By looking at modern society through both of these lenses, however, we can grasp a greater understanding of how bourgeois society reproduces and propagates itself, and how both class conflicts and gender roles aid in this process.

Feminism attacks the social roles which are assigned to men and women without studying the social and economic forces which make these gender roles necessary to the ruling class — this study was undertaken by Marxism. At the same time, Marxism ignores the effects of gender roles and familial structures on class conflicts, and ignores the sexual and familial forces which make these economic structures necessary. Marxism thus finds its complement in the analysis of radical feminism.

Both outlooks challenge the basic assumptions of bourgeois society. The capitalist ideologues speak of "individuals" as an undifferentiated abstraction, and pretend that all individuals are "free and equal", that they all have the same standing in relation to one another. Marx saw through this illusion, and declared that individuals in our society are in fact differentiated into distinct economic classes, which are unequal and unfree. Feminism further points out that there is yet another way in which social individuals are differentiated into classes or divisions — some of the members of society (men) are free, while others (women) are not. Those who wish to overthrow the existing social order must, therefore, pay attention to the manner in which both of these divisions, class and gender, interact and support one another, and how they prop up the bourgeois social order.

The Italian Marxist Antonio Gramsci referred to this interconnecting web of social relationships as a "hegemony". If the current hegemony of the capitalists is to be overthrown, Gramsci concluded, then each of the social relationships which support it must be broken and replaced with new, egalitarian ones.

A vital part of this system of social hegemony, Gramsci pointed out, were gender roles and familial institutions. A socialist revolution was impossible, he wrote, "until women can attain not only a genuine independence in relation to men, but also a new way of conceiving themselves and their role in sexual relations." In contrast to the position of the Leninists, who assert that the liberation of women cannot take place until after the socialist revolution, the council communists conclude that no socialist revolution is possible until patriarchical relationships are first broken. As Batya Weinbaum writes, "Our question then becomes, not 'how do women fit into the revolution', but 'what kind of revolution do women need'."

The focus of the feminist revolution must be the family. As Kate Millett points out, the family structure is an important part of the bourgeois social order: "Mediating between the individual and the social structure, the family affects control and conformity where political and other authorities are insufficient."

Sheila Rowbotham echoes,

> Marxist sociology has tended to concentrate on work relations rather than family relations. The worker's consciousness is seen as developing only at the point of production. It is forgotten that the worker came from a particular family, and that we conceive the world through the relationships of the family, through eyes which grew accustomed to other human beings first in the family.

A workshop at the 1970 Revolutionary People's Convention concluded simply, "The nuclear family is a micro-cosm of the fascist state, where the woman and children are owned by, and their fates determined by, the needs of men, in a man's world."

The bourgeois family is not only the most efficient mechanism for distributing consumer commodities, but also serves a crucial role in maintaining and preserving capitalist relationships. In essence, the family unit has been moved from an economic and productive role to one of social and sexual control. It is no accident that the most pro-business conservatives are also those who yell the loudest for a return to "traditional family values".

The traditional capitalist family serves as a way to preserve the division of labor and the concentration of wealth. Wealthy families can prepare themselves for such privileged economic roles as stockholders, executives and financiers, and can pass on their accumulated wealth to the next generation. Working class families, by contrast, rarely advance in economic position, and have little wealth to pass on to their descendants. This structure tends to stabilize class memberships, to preserve the ruling elite's "old money" and to help prevent the rise of new economic competitors.

Within the working class, traditional family and gender roles play a large part in determining economic position. An unmarried woman is paid the minimum wage at a dead-end job, on the assumption that she only needs a bare minimum to stay alive until she marries and has children. A married man, however, is paid more, since he is expected to be the "breadwinner" for his whole family.

The working class father's traditional role as "breadwinner", moreover, reinforces conservatism and passive acceptance of the existing social order. The head of a family cannot summarily reject a job which is dangerous or unfair, since he must have a source of wage income if he is expected to fulfill his role as husband and father. On the other hand, he cannot become too militant in fighting for his interests against those of the boss, since he can then be fired and lose his source of wage income. If he is to feed his family, the worker must give in to the authority of the owners.

The traditional housewife, at the same time, is forced into a position of economic dependence on her husband. Not only does this reinforce and expand the social and economic obligations of the husband (forcing him to give in to the existing social order), but it also prevents the woman from becoming economically and, as a result, socially, independent. The traditional family also locks the woman into a limited number of social relationships, restricting her horizons to her family and thus impeding the development of a wider social point of view. All of these things help keep women in a subordinate social position.

In the "communist" countries, such as China or the Soviet Union, changes in the ownership of the means of production did absolutely nothing to change any of these debilitating social relationships. Soviet families were still absolutely dependent upon the "breadwinner's" earnings and on familial economic ties, which tended to reproduce all of the inequalities cited above. To combat this, as Shulamith Firestone points out, "We shall need a sexual revolution much larger than — inclusive of — a socialist one to truly eradicate all class systems."

The emancipation of women did not become possible until women gained actual (rather than merely theoretical) access to education and jobs. This didn't happen until the early 1970's, when economic circumstances forced increasing numbers of women into the workforce.

As a result of this and other socio-economic changes, the structures and relationships of the traditional nuclear family have been evolving, and this process of evolution will have a far-reaching impact on other social relationships. "However one defines it," Eisenstein points out, "women's place is integrally embedded in social life. To shift or disrupt it, as has begun to happen in recent years, is potentially to shift and disrupt much else, from personal identity and sexual mores, to family arrangements, child-rearing customs and educational patterns, and from religious ideology to political and economic structures."

The current movement of women into the workforce is providing the economic means for their emancipation. For the first time, women have the potential for real access to enough economic resources to allow them to live free of the economic constraints of the patriarchical family — women can now earn enough to live without being financially dependent upon their husbands. (This economic independence vanishes, however, as soon as a woman has children and can no longer work.)

This liberation of women cannot take place within current patriarchical familial structures or gender roles. Accordingly, traditional bourgeois family structures and gender roles are being increasingly challenged on many fronts, as feminists fight for the independence and self-determination of women in all aspects of their social lives.

There are four basic areas identified by feminists in which radical changes need to be made in order to bring about a feminist revolution. In the sphere of reproductive rights, the goal is to provide women with complete freedom of choice in reproductive matters, free from the interference of men. This area of struggle starts with the fight over abortion and a woman's right to choose what happens to her own body. It also includes the right of access to contraceptives and the ability to decide when or whether a woman chooses to have a child. More radical issues include areas such as artificial reproduction and "test-tube babies". By allowing a woman the opportunity to reproduce independently of men, feminist advances in these areas undermine the restrictions of a patriarchical family consisting of a husband, a wife and their offspring.

Another area that has been targeted by feminist revolutionaries is that of the social integration of women and children. The goal of this struggle is to do away with the traditional family structure and replace it with a society of highly mobile "free-floating" individuals, who are free to enter or leave inter-personal relationships as they please. This fight is also necessary to preserve the economic independence of women who choose to have children. Struggle also centers around issues such as divorce laws, child custody, marriage practices and child care.

The traditional family structure is also being undermined by the movement towards sexual freedom. This movement focuses on family planning and contraception, and also includes the elimination of all laws which limit an individual's sexual freedom — laws against "immoral acts" and the legal obstacles for unmarried couples living together.

The final struggle for women's liberation is in the economic sphere. If women are to be truly independent of familial and gender restrictions, they must have access to sufficient resources to allow them to be economically independent of the family structure. This fight begins with issues such as equal pay for equal work, equal opportunity for economic advancement, and an end to sexual harassment on the job. In the end, this fight will produce far-ranging changes in economic and social structures.

In the final stages of the feminist revolution, the economic independence of women demands a pooling of economic resources on the social level rather than within the nuclear family, so that each individual is capable of economic independence whether they are a part of a family structure or not. It is in this area that socialism and feminism overlap — social distribution of resources cannot take place without the social production of resources. This economic independence cannot be achieved as long as wealth is held by a small class of owners; women's liberation demands a socialist revolution as well as a feminist one.

The National Organization for Women, founded in 1966, is one of the largest feminist organizations in the world, but it is mild, liberal and reformist in nature — i.e., it seeks to allow women to integrate themselves more fully into existing society without seeking to change the basic structure of that society. Such an organization, the radical feminists realize, is incapable of emancipating women.

Many of the liberal reforms being proposed by NOW, in fact, will, without an accompanying change in social institutions, be detrimental to the very women they claim they are helping. A good example is the movement towards easing divorce laws. In a society in which most women are economically dependent upon the wages of the male, divorce is a hollow right. Easier divorce laws can, within existing social circumstances, mean nothing more than a quick re-marriage, since most women cannot remain economically independent on their own. Once again, NOW is demonstrating its traditional concern for the educated upwardly-mobile women who have the means of economic independence, while ignoring the vast majority of working class women.

If a woman's right to a divorce is to mean anything, then women — *all* women — must have easy access to the economic resources which will allow them to live on their own. This cannot be accomplished without drastic changes in the social and economic spheres, changes which go far beyond mere legalistic reforms.

The deep-ranging social, political and economic changes which are necessary for a true feminist revolution cannot, it is obvious, be carried out within the framework of existing patriarchical relationships and institutions. This, then, raises the same question that has faced the socialist movement for so long; how can the movement organize itself to reach its goals without depending upon existing institutions to accomplish this?

There is only one alternative. If women cannot achieve liberation through *existing* relationships and institutions, they must organize *alternative* (even illegal) social relationships and institutions to take their place. It is not enough to reform or alter patriarchical institutions — the key to a successful feminist revolution is to break up these institutions and to build a "dual power" alternative to them.

There are examples of this kind of "direct action". One is the movement towards single-parent families and unmarried couples living together. In the space of a few years, people have built up a huge network of alternative lifestyles that exist alongside of and in competition with the out-dated traditional marriage institution, and which have forced widespread changes in the legal, social and economic structures of industrial society.

Another example is the growth of services such as rape crisis centers and shelters for battered women — issues which are largely ignored by the state, but which serve as the center for women's self-organization. In essence, these women's groups are building a miniature "counter-state", which meets their own needs as those needs are defined by themselves.

Such an aggressive construction of alternative social relationships lies at the heart of the feminist revolution. To win social control of economic resources (and thus economic independence for women), women must organize in the workplace. If women are to safeguard abortion rights and obtain reproductive freedom, they must organize a network to provide this — legally or illegally. If restrictive relationships are to be left behind, then new progressive ones must arise in their place.

The success of the feminist revolution and the establishment of egalitarian gender relationships not only undermines patriarchy, but also all of those oppressive social relationships which are reinforced by patriarchical institutions. Since bourgeois society is dependent upon an interconnecting web of social relationships, the collapse of any one brings with it the possibility of creating a crisis that could collapse the entire structure.

If we are to take advantage of this possibility, however, we must continue to examine the human relationships which make up the bourgeois social order.

Heterosexism

Of all the social inequalities in modern bourgeois society, the repression of lesbians and gays is the most obviously visible. Unlike women, African-Americans or disabled people (all of whom have at least nominal legal protection against discrimination), gays and lesbians have no protection under the law. They can be discriminated against in matters of housing and employment; they can be expelled from military service. They cannot form legal marriages, cannot designate each other as legal next of kin, and cannot will estates to each other. In many states, "anti-sodomy" laws make homosexual acts illegal and punishable by jail terms. Some states require those convicted of "sexual perversion" crimes (including homosexual acts) to register with the local sheriff when they move into a neighborhood.

This repression has historically driven gays and lesbians "into the closet", forcing them to lead secret lives while attempting to pass themselves off as heterosexuals. As gay activist Carl Wittman says, "Our fear of coming out is not totally paranoid; the stakes are high — loss of family ties, loss of jobs, loss of straight friends — these are all risks." It is only within the last twenty years that a real movement for gay liberation has taken root.

In ancient societies such as Greece or Rome, homosexuality (particularly sex between men and boys) was viewed as healthy and normal. It wasn't until the rise of feudal society that severe restrictions were placed on sexual activities. These restrictions — forbidding anal or oral sex and masturbation — were based on strict separation of sex and love; sex was a simple procreative act, while love was an emotional bond which was above any mere desires of the flesh. Thus, the regulation of sexual behavior had less to do with controlling personal relationships than it had with controlling procreative activity. Activities that did not lead to procreation were considered sinful, since God had directed humans to "be fruitful and multiply" (and since feudal society needed an ever-increasing number of serfs to work the fields and defend against invading neighbors).

With the rise of the nuclear family, coinciding with the rise of industrial society, homosexuality was specifically condemned. The nuclear family became the basic unit of the new social order, and its patriarchical and economic relationships were a pillar supporting social stability. Homosexuality flew in the face of this social institution, and was therefore vigorously repressed.

In recent times, issues of homosexuality (fueled by the AIDS crisis) have been framed largely by the right-wing Christian fundamentalists. It is no accident that the word most often used to describe homosexuality — "sodomy" — is derived from Biblical sources. In essence, homophobia and heterosexism serve the same purpose for bourgeois society as religious codes did in feudal society — to maintain the existing social structures.

In feudal society, political and economic power was wielded by the Church, through the doctrines of Divine Right. In this outlook, the universe was fixed in an immutable order by the grace of God, and any attempt to change or alter the existing social order was not only a political crime against the king, but a sin against God and the Church. Those who challenged this accepted view were condemned as heretics and executed by the religious authorities.

Under capitalism, the religious outlook was abandoned in favor of "rationality" and "scientific thought". The necessity for social control was not abandoned, however; it was merely altered in form, and the new science of psychology grew to assume an important place in the bourgeoisie's instruments of social power. Under capitalist society, undesirable or dangerous social behavior, rather than being labeled a "sin", was transformed into a "mental illness". Those who rejected social orthodoxy were no longer "heretics"; they now became "social deviants". Just as the ancient Church had to either convert the heretics to the "true faith" or eliminate them, modern psychology attempts to "cure" the social deviants or, failing that, to "control" their "compulsions".

The process of transforming the methods of social control can be clearly seen in the history of anti-gay repression. In the Middle Ages, those who openly practiced homosexuality were assumed to be witches or agents of Satan, and were burned as heretics. In capitalist society, however, homosexuality has been assumed to be a pathological condition to be treated; gays and lesbians are assumed to be "sick" or "ill". "It has recently been discovered," a 1959 textbook concluded, "that homosexuality is a curable disease."

This outlook produced what psychologist Thomas Szasz called "the manufacture of madness", a psychological debate over the nature of homosexuality that rages, in much the same form, even today, and has been the source of much repression of lesbians and gays. On the one hand are those who argue that homosexuality is a freely-chosen way of life, that people are "recruited" into the gay lifestyle. On the other side are those who argue that homosexuality is genetically inherent in certain people, that gays are "born, not made".

In a very real sense, however, this debate over "nature" or "nurture" is quite irrelevant to gay liberation, since either outlook provides a "scientific" justification for the repression of gays. If homosexuality is a chosen behavior, psychologists argue, then it is necessary to alter or change these behavior patterns to prevent the homosexuals from "spreading" their lifestyle and "recruiting" others. If, on the other hand, homosexuality is genetic, if gays are "born that way", then they are afflicted with an unfortunate "disease" which must be "cured" to make them "normal".

"The question of whether or not homosexuality is an illness," says Szasz, "is therefore a pseudo-problem":

> If by "disease" we mean deviation from an anatomical or physiological norm—as in the case of a fractured leg or diabetes—then homosexuality is clearly not a disease... But even if homosexuals were proven to have certain sexual preferences because of their nature, what would that prove? People who are prematurely bald are sick, in a stricter sense of this word, than homosexuals could possibly be. What of it?

"Clearly," Szasz concludes, "the question that is really being posed for us is not whether or not a given person manifests deviations from an anatomical and physiological norm, but what moral and social significance attaches to this behavior."

In the area of gay and lesbian liberation, medical science has served a patently political role—to repress gays and lesbians and to safeguard existing social institutions. As gay activist Dick Leitsch said in 1967, "When doctors rush into print with wild claims of 'cures' for homosexuality, they are not serving the homosexuals. Indeed, they are doing just the opposite; they are increasing social pressure on him. . . . A 'cure' would be a sort of 'final solution' to the homosexual problem."

Szasz says of those psychologists who want to "cure" gays and lesbians, "His 'therapeutic' recommendations for homosexuality bear out the suspicion that his medical role is but a cloak for that of the moralist and the social engineer."

The role of the medical establishment in the repression of homosexuals became even more visibly apparent after the onset of AIDS. Now, instead of merely viewing homosexuality as a sickness, the medical establishment was able to use a real sickness as a pretext for attacking homosexuality.

Sexually transmitted diseases have always been used as a method of controlling social behavior and reinforcing existing sexual and familial structures. People who left the constraints of the socially-sanctioned nuclear family, by frequenting prostitutes or by promiscuity, ran the risk of syphilis, gonorrhea and chlamydia (or, in the case of women, pregnancy, which in this instance functioned as a disease). As a result, research into the prevention of sexually transmitted diseases or pregnancy (prophylactics, vaccines, contraceptives) has always been virtually ignored, on the grounds that those who got such a condition "deserved it". And, because sexually transmitted diseases are easily treated with antibiotics, not much research into new cures was ever carried out by the medical establishment. It was into these circumstances that AIDS intruded in the 1970's.

In the United States, the initial victims of the AIDS epidemic (male homosexuals, intravenous drug users, Haitian immigrants, and prostitutes) were people whom the social elite views as "expendable" or as potential threats to the existing social structure. As a result, little research was carried out on AIDS for a period of several years. It was not until the virus began to enter the white male heterosexual world, through blood transfusions and sexual contact, that AIDS began to receive serious attention.

The Religious Right was quick to realize the social and political significance of the disease, and seized on AIDS as a convenient ideological tool in their defense of the existing social order. Jerry Falwell, Pat Robertson and their ilk declared that AIDS was a punishment from God, a plague visited upon the homosexual sinners as a punishment for their evil ways. The only "cure" for AIDS, the Right thundered, was to maintain a traditional, monogamous lifestyle.

The fire and brimstone began to flow. The Christian Family Renewal sent out an appeal for funds, declaring, "You may soon fall victim to an irreversible, fatal disease. And it won't be your fault! But you'll have to pay the terrible price anyway because of the promiscuous homosexuals!" Conservatives argued against allowing gays and lesbians to teach in schools or day care centers, declaring that these "perverts" would seduce our children and lead them into a lifestyle of certain death.

The Right wing didn't concern itself with finding a cure for AIDS and opposed any governmental funding to find a treatment for the disease; it was more concerned with preventing the spread of the disease to "healthy" people. AIDS victims such as blood transfusion patients and infected newborns were referred to as "innocent victims of the AIDS crisis" — the implication being that the rest of the AIDS victims were "guilty" and "deserved it". In a similar vein, a Pennsylvania woman who was infected with AIDS by her dentist was brought before a congressional committee to tearfully insist that she had "done nothing wrong". The program of the Right is chilling in its simplicity — prevent the spread of AIDS to "innocent victims" and allow the homosexuals to kill each other off.

In some instances, the reaction of the radical Left to the AIDS crisis was not much better. Several Left groups supported the actions of state officials who closed down the bathhouses which serve as social centers for the gay community, rationalizing that such steps were necessary to halt the spread of AIDS and "save the gays from themselves".

For the most part, the Marxist Left has always ignored the gay and lesbian movement. The Left, writes Cindy Patton, has only a dim understanding of the gay struggle, and as a result, she says, "Lesbian/gay liberation and the straight Left have had a checkered history at best."

Marxist involvement with gay and lesbian issues dates back to 1898, when August Bebel, a Socialist member of the Reichstag, urged the repeal of the Prussian anti-sodomy laws. Marxists Rudolph Hilferding, Karl Kautsky and Eduard Bernstein were among those who signed petitions to repeal the anti-gay laws.

In 1950, American Communist Party member Harry Hay resigned from the Party to form the Mattachine Society, the first openly pro-gay liberation group in the United States.

In the 1960's, in the early stages of the counter-culture movement, many lesbians attempted to find a place within the new feminist movement, but were quickly rebuffed. Most of the mainstream feminist organizations (including NOW) were wary of paying too much attention to lesbian issues for fear of losing "respectability". Feminist liberals fought to keep gay issues separate from the women's struggle for equal access.

At the same time, the radical feminists also looked upon the lesbian movement with suspicion. The New York group Redstockings accused lesbians of "infiltrating" independent women's centers and feminist publications. In May 1970, a delegation of lesbians appeared at the Second Congress to Unite Women wearing lavender T-shirts that proclaimed "Lavender Menace", as a protest against the isolation of gay women within the feminist movement.

After such protests, some feminists gave in. In 1977, Betty Freidan, who had actively purged lesbians from NOW, reversed herself and called for unity within the women's movement. NOW issued a statement acknowledging "the oppression of lesbians as a legitimate concern of feminists".

Some of the most militant lesbian activists were repelled by the open sexism of the male-dominated gay rights movement, and were drawn into the radical feminist "men are the enemy" line. They declared themselves to be "lesbian separatists" and advocated that all women become "political lesbians" — that is, to avoid male-female relationships entirely since they were inherently one-sided and exploitative. The New York group The Feminists, for example, announced, "You can't be a real radical if you don't sleep with women." In the battle of the sexes, the lesbian separatists called for a strategy of "no fraternization with the enemy".

Many Leftist activists viewed the debate over gay liberation and sexual politics as a diversion from the "real goals" of the Movement. While Leftists and liberals of every political stripe accepted that gays and lesbians deserved the civil rights to do whatever they wished, most organizations did virtually nothing to help them in this struggle, and, by limiting the struggle to a mere fight for civil rights, all of them ignored the deeper issues raised by the gay liberation movement.

Several Left organizations were openly hostile to gay liberation. Eldridge Cleaver of the Black Panthers once said that being gay was as bad as being the Chairman of General Motors. Allen Young, of SDS, felt "totally alone as a homosexual". "The traditional Left, both Old Left and New Left," he concluded, "has been as oppressive to homosexuals as has been establishment America."

The Communists, for the most part, viewed the gay struggle as a hedonistic distraction, and asserted that homosexuals should drop their sexual fight and join the working class movement—quietly. Carl Wittman concluded that the Leninists "see us as jeopardizing their 'work' with workers." "Sex," gay activist Cindy Patton sarcastically notes, "is one of those things that will take care of themselves after the revolution; no one is sure how. . . Too much attention to sexuality is petty bourgeois, claim sectarians, baffled by the persistence of this topic. And besides, the workers are too busy for sex." Whenever Marxists spoke of inter-personal relationships, it was assumed as a matter of course that these would be heterosexual.

Many Marxists had trouble viewing gays and lesbians as an oppressed class, and many more simply viewed the oppression of gays as unimportant or secondary. "A lot of 'movement' types," says Wittman, "come on with a line of shit about homosexuals not being oppressed as much as Blacks or Vietnamese or workers or women. We don't happen to fit into their ideas of class or caste." Wittman concluded that the Marxists were out of touch with the gay movement: "Talk about the priority of Black Liberation or ending imperialism over our 'problem' is just anti-gay propaganda."

Allen Young adds:

> Our struggle is denied by straight people who think of themselves as being part of the "broader struggle", who define themselves as the "real revolutionaries". . . Straight leftists will accept

us so long as they can conceive of us as something like "United Homosexuals for Peace, Equality and Socialism".

"I am constantly being coerced," Young says, "gently or arrogantly, to provide a class analysis of homosexuality."

Today, Marxist-Leninist groups still cannot relate to the gay liberation struggle. The Revolutionary Communist Party viewed the lesbian and gay culture as a perversion forced upon people by capitalism, and asserted that, after the Revolution, gays will simply disappear and there will be no more "homosexual question":

> As for homosexuality, this too is perpetuated and fostered by the decay of capitalism, especially as it sinks into deeper crisis. This is particularly the case because of the distorted, oppressive man-woman relationships capitalism promotes. Once the proletariat is in power, no one will be discriminated against in jobs, housing and the like merely on the basis of being a homosexual. But at the same time, education will be conducted throughout society on the ideology behind homosexuality and its material roots in exploiting society, and struggle will be waged to eliminate it and reform homosexuals.

This program should sound familiar; it is nothing more than a return to the old idea that homosexuality is an "aberration" that can be "corrected". The RCP's final solution to gay and lesbian liberation was to "educate" and "reform" (and thus eliminate) gays and lesbians. In 1991, the RCP was expelled from an anti-war coalition in San Francisco because of its anti-gay stance. As a result, the RCP acknowledged its "error" and has since renounced its anti-gay stance.

Other Leninist groups may not be as openly anti-gay as the RCP was, but they have proven to be just as isolated from the gay and lesbian movement. As gay activist Sushwan Robb says:

> Those on the left that rejected the most blatantly homophobic views often held positions that nevertheless seriously belittled the issues of lesbian and gay rights. For instance, some accepted homosexuality as a personal lifestyle (for someone else) but denied that

it was an issue fit for political action, and insisted people keep their sexuality hidden. Others accepted the validity of political struggle for queer rights, but as an issue based on individual rights, and therefore a low priority.

When the Leninists have entered the arena of gay liberation, it is usually with the goal of winning "cadres" for the socialist struggle, leaving gay groups, as Tede Matthews says, "with a deep sense of having been betrayed." Activist Marcy Rein points out that it is "unspeakably frustrating to have the open mike dominated by Trot after Trot ranting about how revolutionary socialism (whatever the hell that means these days) would fix everything."

The various "Marxist-Leninist" nations, moreover, have, in every case, put the RCP's anti-gay sentiments into practice, and have been almost puritanical in their rooting out of gay and lesbian culture. In the aftermath of the 1917 Revolution, the Soviets repealed the Tsarist anti-homosexual laws and announced that gays would no longer be discriminated against or repressed. By 1934, however, this tune had changed, and now homosexuals were being condemned as "decadent" and "bourgeois". Mass arrests took place in Moscow, Odessa and Leningrad, targeting artists, actors and musicians. Those arrested were accused of "homosexual orgies" and received prison terms of five years. During Stalin's purges, homosexuality became an offense almost as repugnant to the Stalinists as Trotskyism.

In Cuba, Fidel Castro considered homosexuality to be a decadent evil of capitalism, and took steps to remove gays from leadership positions. Rolando Cubela, a student leader who had fought in Castro's guerrilla army, was one of many gays who were passed over for a position in the revolutionary government. Cubela responded by joining the CIA-organized attempts to overthrow Castro. By the time of the Bay of Pigs invasion, Cuban gays were being viewed by the ruling Popular Socialist Party as dangerous counter-revolutionary threats. Neighborhood CDRs (Committees for the Defense of the Revolution) were formed to keep an eye out for gays and other counter-revolutionaries.

In 1965, Cuban gays were rounded up and sent to rural "Military Units for the Aid of Production". These UMAP camps lasted for only two years, but produced deep enmity towards the regime among the Cuban gay community. In 1971, the Cuban First National Congress aggravated the situation by calling for the removal of gays from positions as schoolteachers, in an attempt to halt the spread of "bourgeois vices".

The Cubans even screened gays and lesbians from the Venceremos Brigades, the North American solidarity groups that travelled to Cuba to help with the coffee and sugar harvests. This practice wasn't halted until the 1990's, and now gay and lesbian Brigade members are treated to guided tours that show how well homosexuals are treated in the Cuban Socialist Paradise. "Though this marks a definite step forward," says Robb, "some veteran queer solidarity activists remain skeptical of the depth of the change, as the VB has never publicly acknowledged its past homophobic position."

Of all the leftist revolutionary groups, only the African National Congress has been open in its support of gay and lesbian liberation. The constitution prepared by the ANC included a clause specifically acknowledging the rights of gays and lesbians, the only constitution in the world to do so.

Looking at the results of "socialist revolutions" in the USSR and elsewhere, gay and lesbian activists are understandably in no hurry to endorse the same here. As activist Carl Wittman trenchantly points out, "No one — capitalistic or communistic — has treated us as anything other than shit so far."

Rebuffed and disillusioned by the feminists and the socialists, the gay and lesbian community was forced to act alone. The starting point came in June 1969, during a police raid on the Stonewall, a gay bar in New York's Greenwich Village. Police raids on bars had been a fact of gay life for decades, but this time, to the utter shock of the police, the gays fought back. Cars were overturned, police officers were roughed up, and the gay liberation movement was born. In the aftermath of Stonewall, the Gay Liberation Front and the Gay Activists Alliance were formed.

Their 1980's counterparts were the Gay and Lesbian Task Force and the militant Queer Nation and the AIDS Coalition to Unleash Power (ACT UP).

The basic outlook of the militant gay liberation movement can be summed up in the slogan, "Out of the closets, into the streets". "Our first job," writes Carl Wittman, "is to liberate ourselves, and that means clearing our heads of all the garbage that's been poured into them. . . If we are liberated, we are open with our sexuality. Come out, come out, come out." ACT UP and Queer Nation activists are defiantly proud of their identity. A favorite chant goes, "We're here; we're queer. Get used to it."

Until the post-Stonewall movement, gays and lesbians were largely isolated from each other and had virtually no collective social, economic or political power. Now, however, the gay community has gained a greater sense of its identity and potential strength. In some areas, such as parts of San Francisco, Washington DC and New York, gays and lesbians have created their own "ghettoes", virtually self-ruling communities where homosexual culture can be openly practiced.

Lesbian and gay liberation, however, demands more than the establishment of such isolated havens (which cut off gays from influence in the outside world and make repressive "gay-bashing" all the more easier). Real liberation demands the acceptance of homosexuality by the straight world, and the full and free participation of gays and lesbians in all social relationships.

Since the onset of the AIDS crisis, gay and lesbian activists have focused tremendous energies on expanding AIDS research and education, and these efforts have been vital in uniting and radicalizing the gay community. The more moderate gay activists have focused their attention on working within the system, and are attempting to introduce anti-discrimination laws to give gays and lesbians the same legal protections enjoyed by women, Blacks and other minorities. Others are devoting their attention to repealing the various "anti-sodomy" laws found in many states.

Such legal and legislative remedies, however, cannot form the basis for a real liberation of lesbians and gays. Anti-discrimination laws have not greatly improved the positions of women or African-Americans, and there is little reason to believe it would do much better for gays. The repeal of anti-gay laws would also have little effect on the way homosexuals are actually treated on a day-to-day basis. As activist Mark Hoffman points out, the problems which gays face "are, basically, not legal problems. They are social problems of a much more subtle kind, and in order for these problems to be solved, fundamental changes in the public attitude towards homosexuality will have to occur. . . Its ultimate aim must be to bring about substantial changes in society."

The Christian conservatives have seen, as the Leninist Left has not, the danger that gay liberation presents to the established social order. Although the fundamentalists phrase their attacks upon homosexuality in religious and moral terms, it is really a social and political concept they are desperately fighting against.

In many ways, the aims of the gay and lesbian liberation movement are similar to those of the radical feminist movement. Both are fighting for the establishment of free and egalitarian inter-personal relationships. In the gay and lesbian struggle, however, the imperative is much stronger, since homosexuals have rejected the traditional social relationships and have no choice but to operate outside of them. Having already established alternative forms of inter-personal relationships which they need to defend, gays provide living examples of alternative social structures, examples which directly attack and undermine the nuclear family unit — one of the major pillars of bourgeois society.

Feminist challenges to the nuclear family can be kept in check by patriarchical power relationships, but gays and lesbians, who exist outside of this framework, are invulnerable to these checks. It is therefore necessary, from the point of view of the ruling elite, to combat homosexual relationships directly through repression and homophobia. If allowed to run free, the conservatives realize, such a challenge to traditional orthodoxy could easily grow into a wide-ranging movement which attacks the very structure of existing society.

Such a movement deserves the support of any group that is fighting to change the existing social structure. For the most part, however, the Leninists have virtually ignored the lesbian and gay struggle. At best, the Leninists have merely added a phrase or two about "gay liberation" to the long list of things which will happen "after the Revolution", in the socialist Promised Land. At worst, they have attempted to dominate or utilize the gay movement for their own ends, while ignoring the real needs of that movement. As gay activist Angie Fa puts it:

> As we were fighting to win domestic partnerships, where were you? As our community was devastated by AIDS, where were you? As we were trying to win the basic rights to legally protect ourselves from discrimination on the basis of sexual orientation, where were you? As we were fighting to keep our country's borders open to those with HIV, especially to attend conferences or for medical treatment, where were you?

"We gays want and need autonomy," concludes Allen Young, "yet the straight movement continually denies the validity of our struggle. . . The oppression which we suffer from straight society, and our consequent quest for freedom, is the only justification or validation we need."

On the other hand, the gay and lesbian movement has tended to ignore questions involving class or economic issues, and has preferred to view itself as a single harmonious "gay community". As a result, some gay militants have come to accept behavior between gays that would be condemned as outrageous if it involved straights. In September 1992, for instance, when a group of gay labor activists from the Industrial Workers of the World attempted to unionize the End-Up, a gay bar in San Francisco, many local gay activists criticized the effort for "dividing the community". As one Wobbly official said, "The myth of a 'community' is a dangerous smokescreen as long as gay capitalists can exploit their queer workers and then try to smooth things over in the name of 'family'."

It is a mistake to assume, as many gay activists do, that there is a single undifferentiated "gay community". Since most gay activists (like most feminists) are well-off whites, the movement has tended to generalize their outlooks and attempted to apply them to everybody. However, the gay community is subject to as much division among racial, gender and economic lines as any other social grouping. The needs and wants of a young Black gay living in Harlem are not at all the same as those of a wealthy gay stockbroker living in Greenwich Village.

Despite these internal divisions, however, the gay and lesbian struggle for liberation will have far-reaching effects on bourgeois society. As Cindy Patton points out, "As a movement for social change, lesbians and gay men challenge the gender-role structure on which society rests." Carl Wittman urges gays to attack and undermine oppressive social institutions:

> We lived in these institutions all our lives, so naturally we mimic the roles. For a long time, we mimicked these roles to protect ourselves--a survival mechanism. Now, we are becoming free enough to shed those roles which we've picked up from the institutions which have imprisoned us.

Because lesbians and gays are forced to live outside the traditional family structure, they have been free to explore a wide variety of differing inter-personal relationships. This underground social structure produces the same kinds of direct face-to-face human relationships which are the goal of feminism in the familial sphere and of socialism in the economic sphere. "We have to define for ourselves," says Wittman, "a new pluralistic, role-free social structure. It must contain both the physical space and spiritual freedom for people to live alone, live together for a while, live together for a long time, either as couples or in larger numbers."

In particular, the gay and lesbian community has recently been forced, by the AIDS crisis, to depend upon its own resources and meet its own needs through self-organization. When the government refused to undertake the tasks of AIDS education and did little or nothing to support the victims of AIDS, the gay movement was forced to organize its own groups to do these things for themselves. As a result, the gay movement is now realizing its own power, and has gained practical experience in organizing to assert that power.

Currently, the gay and lesbian movement, like the feminist movement, suffers from severe limitations. The most crippling is the lack of a radical vision—a program for real self-organization and self-liberation, and a practical strategy to implement it. For the most part, the largest and most influential gay and lesbian groups have called for nothing more than the full integration of gays into the existing social structure. Few gay activists have openly called for the destruction of existing social institutions and their substitution by new institutions and relationships, ones that have been tailor-made by gays to fit their own needs.

Until this step is taken, the radical gay and lesbian movement will remain limited in its influence. Until gays begin to question the very nature of the social relationships into which they seek access, they will be at most a nuisance to the ruling elite, one that can be "bought off" relatively cheaply with a few cosmetic concessions.

Racism

For the most part, Marx's writings concerning race and ethnicity accurately reflected the Victorian era in which he lived. There is a readily discernible streak of Eurocentrism running through most of Marx's writings.

Though himself of Jewish ancestry, Marx was not above using racial and ethnic epithets in his often vitriolic arguments with those who disagreed with him. Marx once referred to his chief opponent, the German socialist Ferdinand Lasalle, as a "Jewish nigger":

> He is descended from the Negroes who joined Moses's exodus from Egypt (unless his paternal mother or grandmother was crossed with a nigger). Well, this combination of Jewish and Germanic stock with the Negroid basic substance is bound to yield a strange product. The fellow's importunity is also nigger-like.

Engels, in turn, referred to Lasalle as a "true Jew" and "a stupid Yid".

On the other hand, Marx praised the American Civil War as a crusade to abolish slavery, and even wrote a letter to Abraham

Lincoln congratulating him on his actions to free Black slaves. Engels, in 1851, wrote to a friend that he hoped "the current persecution of Jews in Germany will spread no further".

In his most extensive treatment of racial and ethnic factors, entitled *On the Jewish Question*, Marx argued for an end to racial and ethnic discrimination, and castigated the capitalist state for its inability to do this. Rather than working to eliminate the conditions for racism, Marx wrote, the capitalist state merely washes its hands of the problem by passing high-sounding legalities:

> It abolishes, after its fashion, the distinctions established by birth, social rank, occupation, when it decrees that birth, social rank, education and occupation are non-political distinctions, that every member of society is an equal partner in popular sovereignty. . . Far from abolishing these effective differences, it only exists insofar as they are presupposed.

Political solutions within the state apparatus, Marx argued, could not change anything unless these actual social relationships themselves were altered. Giving Jews the legal right to vote and run for office, for instance, doesn't change the social subordination of Jews unless the social relationships which restrict their access to education and opportunity are also done away with. By abolishing anti-Semitism legally, the state does nothing to abolish it in practice. Furthermore, leaving these social structures intact insures that anti-Semitism will continue to impact the state and society, despite legalities to the contrary.

For the most part, however, Marx considered race to be an "economic factor", and most of his writings on racial and ethnic conflict center around the its impact on the economic struggle between workers and capitalists. To Marx, race was an important factor only because it created a division within the working class, and prevented workers from uniting to fight their common enemy — the owners. Marx points out:

> English worker hates the Irish worker as a competitor who lowers wages and the standards of life. He feels national and religious

antipathies towards him. He regards him somewhat like the poor whites of the Southern states in North America regard their black slaves. This antagonism among the proletarians of England is artificially nourished and supported by the bourgeoisie. It knows that this split is the true secret of maintaining its power.

"Labor," Marx concluded, "cannot emancipate itself in the white skin when in the black it is enslaved."

This basic rationale, that racism is simply the result of capitalist efforts to divide the working class, runs through most of current Marxist-Leninist thought. Writer Steven Shulman notes:

Marxism locates the source of racism in the efforts of the capitalist class to maximize their profits and power. Racism is conceived instrumentally, as something which the capitalists do to the workers. It is a functionalist approach insofar as it proceeds from effect to cause; racism results in a divided working class, therefore racism is created in order to divide the working class.

Socialist Workers Party organizer Andrew Pulley echoes, "Racism is perpetuated to prevent white and Black workers from getting together to solve these problems."

Thus, the basic thrust of socialist and Marxist thought has been to urge "unity" between Blacks and white workers. In 1921, Communist Party organizer Rose Pastor Stokes declared, "Insofar as you are one with us, the white workers of the world, there is a class conflict coming in the world, and this conflict today overshadows every other element in the conflict of peoples and races and humanity. We must stand together as workers." In the 1960's, the CP was calling for efforts to "work for the unity of white and Negro workers, for a labor—Negro alliance."

In the 1990's, the RCP was still saying, of African-American struggles:

The struggle for equality and emancipation is bound by a thousand links with the struggle of the working class for socialism. . . The forging of the alliance between these two forces, around a program only realizable through and serving the proletarian revolution, will be the key to the victory of the socialist revolution in this country.

The Progressive Labor Party echoes:

> The key to revolution in the United States lies within the interlocking interests in the Black Liberation movement and the working class struggle for socialism.

Historically, however, the relationship between African-Americans and the labor movement has been erratic and, most often, hostile. During the union movements of the 1910's and 1920's, picket lines were often crossed by Blacks who were imported from the South specifically as strikebreakers—a practice encouraged by many Black leaders who saw this as the only way for African-Americans to gain employment in the "white" trades.

The militant labor movement attacked this practice. In 1918, the leftist Black activist Chandler Owen wrote:

> We see Dr. DuBois and all the other Negro editors herald in big headlines "Negroes Break Strike!", as if that were something to exalt in. And they preach a gospel of hate of labor unions in criminal ignorance of the trend of the modern working world, when they should be explaining to Negroes the necessity of allying themselves with the workers' motive power and weapon—the labor union and the strike.

African-American activists responded by pointing to the racism that ran rampant within the labor movement and many of the elements of the socialist movement. Ernest Mair wrote bitterly, "These same Socialists are eloquent in their preachments about the unfairness of the capitalists, and the injustice of being overfed while others starve, but if you think they are talking about the Negro, then you have another guess coming." W.E.B. DuBois bluntly declared, "Socialism for fifty years has been dumb on the Negro problem." Even Chandler Owen was forced to admit, "It is not facetious to state that many Negroes understand the term 'closed shop' to mean 'closed to Negroes'."

The Machinists Union was just one of many who explicitly excluded Blacks from membership. In 1920, the constitution of the union asserted, "Each member agrees to introduce into this union no one but a sober, industrious white man." Only the Industrial Workers of the World ("Wobblies") actively recruited African-American workers into the union movement during the 1920's, and built up a power base in the Philadelphia shipyards under the leadership of Ben Fletcher.

Until the legal end of racial segregation in the 1950's, most unions refused to admit Blacks, or admitted them only into segregated locals. As late as 1963, the AFL-CIO refused to endorse the civil rights March on Washington.

In contrast to the views of the Marxists that Black and white workers should fight together for their common interests, most militant African-American activists have concluded that the racial interests of Black and white workers are in continual conflict. As W.E.B. DuBois put it:

> While Negro labor in America suffers because of the fundamental inequities of the whole capitalist system,the lowest and most fatal degree of its suffering comes not from the capitalists, but from fellow white laborers. It is white labor that deprives the Negro of his right to vote, denies him education, denies him affiliation with trade unions, expels him from decent houses and neighborhoods, and heaps upon him the public insults of open color discrimination.

Today, Black activists still point out that the Communist program of "worker unity" founders on the hard reality of racism, and that Marxists have ignored the very real effects of racial and ethnic institutions upon economics. As South African activist Steven Biko put it:

> Even the most down-trodden white worker still has a lot to lose if the system is changed. He is protected by several laws against competition at work from the majority. He has a vote and he uses it to return the Nationalist Government to power because he sees them as the only people who, through job reservation laws, are bent on looking after his interests against competition with the "natives". . . It immediately kills all suggestions that there could ever be effective rapport between the real workers, i.e., Blacks, and the privileged white

workers, since we have shown that the latter are the greatest supporters of the system. . . Hence, the greatest anti-Black feeling is to be found amongst the very poor whites whom the Class Theory calls upon to be with Black workers in the struggle for emancipation.

American writer Steven Shulman points out that the Marxian equation of "anti-racism" with the "economic interests of workers" simply is not true:

> Let us assume that the traditional Marxists are correct, that racism divides the working class and reduces their bargaining power, and thereby the wage incomes, of white as well as Black workers. Let us also recognize that wages are not the only interests of workers. Employment is another interest. Given that capitalism recurrently creates slack labor markets, job security is a legitimate area of concern for workers. Discrimination reduces the competition for jobs for white workers; hence the existence of a racial hiring queue increases their employment security.
>
> If racism shifts income from all Blacks to all whites, and if capitalists gain proportionately more than white workers, then racism will raise the standard of living of all white workers, even though it also increases inequality between white workers and capitalists.

In other words, racism in the workplace divides the workers and lowers wage levels, thus helping the bosses, but it also helps white workers gain job security and rapid advancement. Racism, far from being inimical to the economic interests of white workers, can be seen to play a large role in protecting them. As writer R. Williams points out:

> Whites' primary concerns are often short-term material well-being in the context of existing capitalist social relations and an uncertain future. Under these conditions, it may well be that whites as a group believe they can more easily protect their economic interests by actively eliminating Black competition than by interracial coalitions.
>
> Thus, the economic conditions of white workers and African-American do not of necessity draw them together. Instead, it presents white workers with a choice—either racial alliance and democratic revolution, or a "proto-fascist" racial separation.

Orlando Patterson writes:

The proto-fascist scenario calls for the containment of the Black poor in concentrated areas and the use of their labor for the menial but still essential tasks that will remain even in the most highly-advanced, post-industrial Utopia.

The clearest examples of this "proto-fascism" can be seen in the apartheid system in South Africa and the ghettoization and de facto segregation in the United States.

Thus, contrary to the assertions of the Leninists, the economic circumstances of the working class do not lead inexorably to a united struggle for socialism. Rather, white workers who fear economic competition from African-American and other ethnic workers more often turn to the "David Duke" solution. The greatest support for the Ku Klux Klan, neo-Nazis, and right-wing "conservative" racist programs such as the dismantling of affirmative action and the abolition of welfare, comes not from the wealthy industrialists, but from the white working class.

This economic factor is openly acknowledged by the racist organizations in the United States. In June 1986, the KKK began a highly publicized campaign to patrol the borders of Texas to keep illegal aliens from entering the country. The purpose of the campaign, said Grand Dragon Charles Lee, was to prevent the foreigners from taking jobs away from American workers. In the 1990's, the White Aryan Resistance began distributing leaflets declaring:

A Challenge to White People
Are you tired of:
--"Affirmative Action" quotas that discriminate against whites in hiring, promotion and admission to colleges and graduate schools?
--A non-enforced immigration policy that allows millions of illegal immigrants each year to flood our country, taking away jobs, consuming vital resources, and taking over politically? . . .
If so, why not join with thousands of your White kinsmen who are looking out for WHITE interests?

In 2006, racism was a profound motive behind various "conservative" efforts (supported largely by the white working class) to restrict immigration and to marginalize "illegal immigrants" – including the construction of a security fence along the US-Mexico border.

The "economic interests" of white workers, then, may lead either to socialism or fascism, depending upon the racial attitudes of the white workers. Still preaching the Leninist's gospel that all workers have common interests, Marxists have utterly failed to recognize that the separate dynamic of racism can act in the material interests of the white worker just as it does the white boss, and that racial relationships have a far-reaching impact upon the economic struggle. Racism is not exclusively created by the capitalists, nor does it exclusively benefit the capitalists.

Most Marxists answer this argument by declaring that the white workers simply are not "class conscious" and do not understand where their "real" interests lie. John Rey, for instance, writes, "The persistence of groupings based on race and ethnicity may sometimes be viewed as a transient form of false consciousness, which will be superseded in due time by true class consciousness."

We will consider the Leninist notion of "false consciousness" in more detail in another chapter. For now, the point to be made is that the Marxist assertion that racism is an ideology imposed upon the workers by capitalist economic interests does not stand up to scrutiny, and is undermined by racial as well as economic arguments.

Further, the Marxist-Leninists have proven themselves completely unable to view racism as a separate and independent social relationship, one which, while having an effect on economic relationships, does not have its root basis in them. Economics, as African-American activists have pointed out, plays an important role in the purely racial function of keeping ethnic minorities in a disadvantaged social position.

In the traditional Marxist analysis, African-Americans and other ethnic minorities are railroaded, using racist methods, by the capitalists into second-class, low-wage jobs. This, the Leninists conclude, produces two benefits for the capitalist; the low-wage Blacks produce a higher rate of profit than would better-paid white workers, and the "surplus army" of African-Americans, through competition with higher-paid whites, helps to keep the general level of wages lower than it would otherwise be.

African-American activists, however, have pointed out two obvious flaws in this argument. First, low-wage Blacks tend to be channeled into small labor-intensive companies with little capitalization. The resulting low rate of productivity insures low wages for any worker, and thus hiring African-Americans produces no higher profit levels than would hiring anybody else. Secondly, since Blacks are racially excluded from most of the high-paying jobs held by whites, there is in reality very little wage competition between them — African-Americans play only a minor role in keeping wage levels down.

Rather than being herded into low-wage jobs for reasons of economic profitability, Black activists point out, it is far more fruitful to conclude that African-Americans are railroaded into dead-end, power-less jobs in order to keep them socially and politically marginalized by limiting their economic power. Economics can thus be usefully studied as merely another way in which whites keep Blacks and other ethnic minorities in an inferior social position. Rather than economics producing racism, racism can be seen to produce specific corresponding economic relationships.

By asserting that African-Americans and white workers have common interests, the Marxist-Leninists have also completely ignored the very real class and social differences within the Black community, and have instead abstracted all African-Americans as "workers", as, says Black activist Harold Cruse, "a people without classes or differing class interests":

American Marxists . . . have no more been able to see the Negro as having revolutionary potentialities in his own right, than European Marxists could see the revolutionary aspirations of their colonials as being independent of, and not subordinate to, their own.

The attitude of most Leninists to the Black Liberation struggle is summed up by writer Wilson Record:

The real differences among men were economic rather than social, racial or psychological. Differences of the latter kinds were superficial and momentary, deriving from the more basic economic forces operating over the course of history. Unity of the proletariat was assured by common suffering under capitalist oppressors; as the exploitation increased, workers would come to realize that the enemy was not members of other racial, nationality or religious groups,but capitalists of whatever identity or persuasion: consequently, there was no need for special concern about racial minorities, including the Negro, in the building of a party that would challenge and triumph over the dominant economic class. Why develop special strategies and approaches to Negroes or other racial minorities, who would certainly join the struggle in the normal course of events?

Because of its denial of African-American efforts to achieve economic and social power as African-Americans, Cruse, one of the most vocal Black critics of Communism, sees Marxism essentially as "a European (white) revolutionary doctrine meant primarily to liberate white workers, leaving non-whites to shift for themselves":

No matter how vocal the Communists were, for example, on "Negro rights", in the final analysis they looked upon the white labor movement as the dominant factor and considered Negroes as merely an appendage in their strategy and tactics.

The "white man's burden" shifts from the capitalist's missionaries to the socialist's revolutionaries, whose duty to history is to lift the "backward" peoples from their ignominious state to socialist civilization—even if whites have to postpone this elevation abroad until they have managed to achieve it at home.

They cannot let go of the *idee fixe* of the white working class "saving" the world's humanity.

Steven Biko, another outspoken critic of Marxism-Leninism, adds:

> These self-appointed trustees of Black interests boast of years of experience in their fight "for the rights of Blacks". They have been doing things for Blacks, on behalf of Blacks and because of Blacks. When the Blacks announce that the time has come for them to do things for themselves and all by themselves, all white liberals shout blue murder! . . . These in fact are the greatest racists, for they refuse to credit us with any intelligence to know what we want.
> They tell us that the situation is a class struggle rather than a racial one. . . We believe that we know what the problem is, and we will stand by our findings.

Throughout the history of the socialist movement, Marxists have shown considerably less enthusiasm for aiding the Black struggle than they have in recruiting Blacks to aid in the socialist struggle; in their eyes, Blacks exist to fight for the Communists rather than the other way around. During the Second World War, the Communist Party preached racial unity and common struggle. This did not prevent the CP, however, from demanding that African-American leaders put their demands on hold until after the war, so that racial conflict would not cripple the war production that was going to aid the beleaguered Soviet Union.

Marxist-Leninist parties today still talk about the role that African-Americans are to play in the socialist revolution, but seldom speak of what the revolution can do for Blacks. The Socialist Workers Party says:

> The present tasks of the SWP in connection with the Negro struggle for liberation are . . . to expand and strengthen the Party's cadre and forces in the Negro organizations and the civil rights movement, by (a) recruiting revolutionary Negroes and helping to train them for leadership in the Party and mass movements.

"It is the task of revolutionary Marxists," the SWP concluded, "to seek to win the best elements of this newly-emerging vanguard to Trotskyism."

The Progressive Labor Party declares, "The Black liberation struggle should be organized nationwide with a variety of mass organizations of, by, and for Black people—emerging, developing, and uniting into a Black Liberation Front led by Black class-conscious revolutionaries."

In order to increase its appeal to Blacks, the Marxist parties soon began to claim militant Black leaders as their own. The Communist Party and the Socialist Workers Party have both glorified W.E.B. DuBois as a revolutionary African-American leader, while castigating the less-militant but more-popular Booker T. Washington as a "class collaborationist". The SWP has also attempted to claim Malcolm X for itself, and has published several volumes of Malcom's speeches (none of which had anything to do with Communism or Marxism). Groups like the SWP and the RCP have also attempted to appeal to African-American militants by running Blacks as candidates for President. Howard Cruse points out that all of this is simply an attempt by white militants to gain control over the Black movement: "The deeply ingrained paternalism of the white radical prompts him to attempt to pick the Negro's heroes out of history for him." Steven Biko echoes, "True to their image, the white liberals always knew what was good for the Blacks and told them so."

This same trend is apparent in the white radical's penchant for selecting certain African-Americans as the "spokesperson" or "leader" of the Blacks, everyone from Martin Luther King to Malcolm X to Louis Farrakhan to Jesse Jackson. The racist assumption behind this, that this or that person can be held to speak for "all Blacks", can best be illustrated by the reaction of these same radicals if someone stood up claiming to speak for "all whites" or "all Americans".

Given the Marxist emphasis on class rather than race, many African-American activists have concluded that socialism is simply irrelevant to the Black movement. Says Cruse:

> Desiring to see the Negro group merely as an appendage to the main body of white workers, the Marxists have been unable,

theoretically and practically, to set the Negro off and see him in terms of his own national minority group existence and identity, inclusive of his class, caste and ideological stratifications.

Many of the Leninists, in their arguments for racial solidarity, have not looked beyond the confines of the workplace, and do not take any account of the institutional racism that pervades life outside the factory walls. The Marxists tend to look at all Blacks as oppressed workers, a viewpoint that Cruse calls "the myth of a uniform 'Negro People'." "In reality," he notes, "no such uniformity exists. There are class distinctions among Negroes, and it is misleading to maintain that the interests of the Negro working and middle classes are identical." The Leninists fail to realize that Black professionals, Black businessmen and Black property owners are still oppressed as Blacks, and that racism does not apply only to workers.

The basic thrust of the Communist view of racism is that African-Americans should give up their struggle for the economic and social advancement of their race, and instead join the working class movement. "This," points out Cruse, "is the same as saying that the Negro bourgeoisie had no right to try to become capitalists — an idea that makes no historical sense whatsoever."

The Black Liberation Movement, Cruse points out, has "introduced another factor in revolutionary politics, the racial factor, which Western Marxists never admitted should be a factor of any importance at all."

Workers, in their opinion, regardless of race and national differences, should all think alike on the question of capitalism and imperialism. The Trotskyists still function under this grand illusion.

White capitalists are a catastrophe we hard-pressed, ernest Marxists have to put up with in the course of honorable struggle for socialism. But Black capitalists? My God! (Negroes in America are predominantly workers, the Marxists protest; they are poor people. Other corollaries to this attitude are (1) don't let Negroes get hold of money, that means power, (2) keep all Negroes poor and, therefore, tractable, (3) rich Negroes are an abomination, (4) money spoils Negroes because they don't know how to handle it, (5) all Negroes —

rich and poor—should reject capitalist ambitions in favor of socialist brotherhood, etc., etc., etc.).

All of these Marxian and un-Marxian racial attitudes we American Negroes understand very well. All the folklore of American race prejudice is familiar to us. But it is disastrously appalling when Marxists fall into this mythic pattern of thought.

Nowhere did the Marxist attitude towards class differences in the African-American community become clearer than in the conflict over "integration".

The earliest mass organization to fight for Black liberation, the National Association for the Advancement of Colored People (NAACP) followed a strategy of integration. Far from being a radical or revolutionary group, the NAACP fought for such "middle-class" goals as equal voting rights, equal access to education, and equal business opportunities. Such mild goals hardly posed a threat to the social order, and in fact had a pacifying effect on Black militancy, since the more real gains such a movement was able to win for African-Americans, the larger was their stake in maintaining the existing order of things and their ever-increasing role within it.

In the 1920's, however, a new and more militant Black movement arose, led by the Jamaican-born Marcus Garvey. Garvey asserted that Blacks would never be free in the United States, and advocated the establishment of a separate Black nation in the African homeland. Rather than integration, Garvey and the other Black Nationalists fought for complete separation and an independent Black nation.

The Communists criticized the NAACP as a "bourgeois reformist" group, but their most vehement attacks were reserved for Garvey's "Back to Africa" movement. The CP urged African-Americans to give up their national struggle and join the "real fight"—that between labor and capital. "From the point of view of Marxism," the Party declared, "Negro bourgeois nationalism is reactionary. Proletarian internationalism and Negro bourgeois nationalism are irreconcilable ideologies. They are in conflict, and either one or the other must triumph. They cannot exist side by side."

In the 1980's, writer Earl Ofari echoed:

> Black nationalism, including "revolutionary nationalism", is reactionary and does nothing but retard the struggle. Nationalism often leads to alliances with some of the most backward elements in the Black community. There can never be a principled "all-class" unity with Black millionaires, politicians, police officials, businessmen, professionals, etc., on the part of true revolutionaries.

The Marxist attitude was clear: "true revolutionaries" did not form alliances with "backward elements", and African-American attempts at independence must be resisted in favor of a worker-Black alliance for socialism.

By 1928, however, the Communist Party was forced to admit that the popularity of Garvey's Black Nationalism had overshadowed its own message of racial unity. The CP, as Wilson Record writes, promptly flip-flopped in its attitude to the nationalists:

> They declared that Negroes in the country constituted a nation, and that their exploitation was part and parcel of the same capitalist imperialism which crushed other colored peoples underfoot in Asia and Africa. Therefore, it was argued, a solution of the Negro problem in the United States could be found in the doctrines on minorities, imperialism and nationalism developed by Lenin and presumably applied by the USSR in dealing with Russian racial and cultural minorities.

Now, the struggle for Black Nationalism could be viewed by the Leninists as an "anti-colonialist rebellion" — African-Americans constituted an "internal colony" that could only be freed through a struggle for "national liberation".

The Leninist attitude towards Black Nationalists changed overnight. The Communist Party began calling for an independent Black Republic in the southern states. The SWP began publishing the speeches of Malcolm X and referring to the "special problems of the oppressed nationalities", and declared: "As Black people, through struggle, gain an understanding that self- determination can only be won through the construction of a workers' state, they will come to join the ranks of the multinational revolutionary socialist party."

> We therefore welcome and look forward to the independent mobilization and organization of Black people. The greater the independent organization of Black people, the easier it will be for Black people to acquire socialist consciousness.

Of course, the Leninists were quick to point out, this Black Nation would be "transitional" — that is, it would be expected to defend and embrace the socialist vision of the Marxist-Leninists, and to eventually give way to the exclusive reign of the Leninist state. As one writer points out, "For many Negroes, the proposal of a separate nation sounded like a red-winged Jim Crow."

It was not until the late 1960's that an independent Black Nationalist movement formed, one that rejected Marxist control in favor of "Black Power". In 1966, SNCC led the charge by declaring, "We reject the American dream as defined by white people, and must work to construct an American reality defined by Afro-Americans." SNCC expelled whites from decision-making roles within the organization, a move decried by Marxists and white liberals alike.

In essence, Black Power was a call for Black economic self-determination and social independence, an echo of Garvey's call to "Buy Black". The movement accepted the argument of Booker T. Washington that African-Americans must gain economic independence and control over their own community before they could gain enough real strength to challenge whites for social or political power.

The most well-known of the Black Power groups was the Black Panthers, who preached Black Nationalism but who used Marxist-Leninist verbiage to make their arguments. Despite all of the militant Leninist rhetoric, the Panthers were essentially a nationalist group, fighting for Black control and self-determination in those areas in which African-Americans had a majority of the population.

The Panthers were crushed by fierce police repression, but by that time many American Marxists had already given up their commitment to Black Nationalism and began again calling for integration. Black Nationalism, they concluded, would lead to the strengthening of Black business owners and other "backwards bourgeois elements". The true solution to racial independence, the Leninists now asserted, lay in an alliance with the radical workers and integration within a socialist state.

Many militant Blacks viewed the new shift towards integration as merely another ploy by the Leninists to assert control over the Black struggle. Steven Biko, listening to the South African white radicals expressing their undying devotion to the Black cause, was not impressed:

> These are the people who argue that they are not responsible for white racism and the country's "inhumanity to the Black man". These are the people who claim that they too feel the oppression just as acutely as the Blacks, and therefore should be jointly involved in the Black man's struggle for a place under the sun. In short, these are the people who say that they have Black souls wrapped up in white skins.
>
> Nowhere is the arrogance of the liberal ideology demonstrated as well as in their insistence that the problems of the country can only be solved by a bilateral approach involving both Black and white... As a result, the integration achieved is a one-way course, with the whites doing all the talking and the Blacks the listening.
>
> Instead of involving themselves in an all-out attempt to stamp out racism from their white society, liberals waste lots of time trying to prove to as many Blacks as they can find that they are liberal... White liberals must leave Blacks to take care of their own business, while they concern themselves with the real evil in our society — white racism... No true liberal should feel any resentment at the growth of Black Consciousness. Rather, all true liberals should realize that the place for their fight for justice is within their white society.

If African-Americans and other racial minorities are ever to free themselves, the Black Nationalists say, they must systematically strengthen themselves for an attack on all of the social institutions which hold them back. And, Howard Cruse points out, in the Black community, the most basic problem is the lack of self-determination, which is a direct result of the Black's lack of economic power:

> The Negro is politically compromised today because he owns nothing. He can exert little political power because he owns nothing... In capitalist society, an individual or group that does not own anything is powerless.
>
> Thus, to fight for Black Liberation is to fight for his right to own.

Biko echoes:

> Being part of an exploitative society in which we are often the direct objects of exploitation, we need to evolve a strategy towards our economic situation... Capitalistic exploitative tendencies, coupled with the overt arrogance of white racism, have conspired against us.
>
> We therefore need to take another look at how best to use our economic power, little as it may seem to be. We must seriously examine the possibilities of establishing business cooperatives whose interests will be plowed back into community development programs... "Black man, you are on your own."

Such a program is, of course, anathema to the Marxist groups, who urge Blacks to reject working within the capitalist system and instead join white workers in the fight for socialist revolution. As Howard Winant notes, "The impulse is still very strong to treat racial inequality as a problem of class, thus attempting once more the articulation that has failed so often in the past." Harold Cruse concludes that Marxism has become isolated and irrelevant to Black Liberation, saying, "The failure of American capitalist abundance to help solve the crying problems of the Negro's existence cannot be fobbed off on some future socialist haven."

Instead, as Howard Winant and Michael Omi argue, it is now necessary to examine "the process by which social, economic and political forces determine the content and importance of racial categories, and by which they are in turn shaped by racial meanings. . . . Crucial in this formulation is the treatment of race as a central axis of social relations, which cannot be subsumed under or reduced to some broader category or conception."

Some Marxists are finally beginning to view racism as an independent system with a dynamic of its own, one that is not a mere function of economic exploitation. As writer Steven Shulman concludes, "Race can be interpreted as a self-sustaining hierarchy of status and power which partially constitutes and is partially constituted by class relations."

The Black Liberation movement, however, remains central to any attempts at larger social change. As Cruse points out:

> The Negro movement represents an indirect challenge to the capitalist status quo, not because it is programmatically anti-capitalist, but because full integration of the Negro in all levels of American society is not possible within the present framework of the American system.

At the same time, racial and ethnic activists have realized that the liberal reform movements of the past are not sufficient to gain racial liberation. "American society," concludes Orlando Patterson, "has reached the limits of reformism in its handling of the problem of the Black poor."

The civil rights movement has made significant gains in integrating many racial and ethnic minorities into mainstream society (though, as the recent Los Angeles riots demonstrated, large sectors of the African-American and Latin communities remain hopelessly isolated), but these civil rights gains have been extremely limited and have done little to promote racial self-determination. "Power cannot be wielded," Cruse says, "from integrated lunch counters, waiting rooms, schools, housing, baseball teams or love affairs, even though these are social advances."

The question facing the Black Liberation movement, Cruse concludes, has now become, "How can the Negro movement have the power in and of itself to enforce structural and administrative changes in this capital — labor combination in order to make room for the democratic participation of the Negro?"

Programs of affirmative action and integration cannot accomplish this task — they can provide individual escape, but cannot raise the position of the race as a whole. To accomplish this, racial minorities must make a "racial revolution" to gain self-determination and real independence.

The Black Nationalist programs of economic self-help and self-organization are the key to gaining independence. African-Americans and other racial or ethnic minorities are indeed an "internal colony" within the United States, but their liberation, unlike that of foreign neo-colonies, cannot take the form of "national liberation". In the absence of a defined national land area and national resources, racial liberation depends upon racial economic independence and self-organization. Racial minorities must therefore carry out their own "cultural revolutions" to gain a measure of control over their own economic and social circumstances.

The best-organized step in this direction was the Black Panther program of free breakfasts for schoolchildren and in organizing armed "self-defense" teams to follow the police and intervene whenever civil rights were being violated. These were areas in which the white power structure had shown little interest, and in which African-Americans were able to form their own independent organizations. In essence, such self-organizations function as "mini-states", organized by and for Black people. They point the way to real independence from white power structures.

Steven Biko, in the South African Black Consciousness movement, echoed many of the conclusions of the Black Nationalists. Biko points out that no alliance between Black militants and white radicals will ever be a real "alliance" unless both partners have equal power, influence and decision-making ability. Because whites in South Africa are blessed, whether willingly or not, with more wealth, power and resources than Blacks, any attempt at unity between the two will invariably lead to the domination of the weaker partner by the more powerful. Even with the best of intentions, the white radicals will inevitably take over the organization and play the key roles in decision-making.

The only way to prevent this, Biko declared, was for Blacks to withdraw from such partnerships until they become sufficiently strong on their own to stand with the white radicals on an equal footing, able to formulate and control their own struggle. "What Black Consciousness seeks to do," Biko explained, "is to produce at the output end of the process real Black people who do not regard themselves as appendages to white society." Once that has happened, Blacks will finally be in the position when "we as Blacks must articulate what we want, and put it across to the white man, and from a position of strength say, 'This is what we want.'"

In this struggle for independence, Biko realized, it is the lack of economic resources which most cripples the movement. Therefore, like Howard Cruse in the US, Biko argued that Blacks in South Africa must pool their meager economic resources and utilize them for the benefit of the race, instead of allowing the whites to siphon them off:

> As the situation stands today, money from the Black world tends to take a unidirectional flow to the white society. . . If then we wish to make use of the little we have to improve our lot, it can only lead to a greater awareness of the power we wield as a group. The "Buy Black" campaign that is being wages by some people in the Johannesburg area must not be scoffed at.

Ultimately, however, Biko realized that the only way for Blacks and other racial minorities to obtain economic self-determination is through the equitable access of every individual to the vast economic resources now controlled by the ruling elite. As Biko says:

> It will not be long before Blacks relate their poverty to their Blackness in concrete terms. Because of the tradition forced onto the country, the poor people shall always be Black people. It is not surprising, therefore, that the Blacks should wish to rid themselves of a system that locks up the wealth of the country in the hands of the few.
> In South Africa now there is such an ill distribution of wealth that any form of political freedom which does not touch on the proper distribution of wealth will be meaningless.

It is in this area that the programs of the socialists and racial activists can overlap. Racial minorities must actively seek to build up their own independent power structures within white society, in an effort to gain equal power with white America, but ultimate economic independence will necessitate the seizure and distribution of the vast wealth held by the white business elites. Thus, the racial revolution must at the same time grow into a socialist revolution.

Native Societies

Recent events in the United States and Mexico have focused the attention of the Left on what used to be known as the "national question". The struggles of the Chippewa nation in Wisconsin to maintain its tribal traditions and its sovereign treaty rights concerning spearfishing on Lac du Flambeau, and the armed conflicts which have recently taken place in the Mexican state of Chiapas have once again brought to the fore the problems facing occupied and captive native peoples.

In many ways, the struggles of the native peoples may seem to be akin to those of African-Americans, Latinos, Asian-Americans or other ethnic minorities. From this point of view, white liberals and radicals examine the situation of Native American nations as a subspecies of racial oppression—the programs and outlooks relevant to Black Liberation, these radicals assert, could be easily generalized to include all "people of color". "They have not wanted to show their ignorance about Indians," concludes Lakota activist Vine Deloria. "Instead, they prefer to place all people with darker skin in the same category of basic goals, then develop their programs to fit these preconceived ideas."

During the 1960's, white liberals and radicals consistently urged the Native Americans to become more "militant", to participate in the civil rights movement and to build up "Red Power".

Native activists rejected this outlook, and argued that their situation was very different from that of the racial minorities. The basic thrust of the civil rights movement was to integrate African-Americans more fully into American society; to, in essence, legally eliminate the differences between whites and Blacks. Native tribes, however, were in the opposite situation—they had historically existed as separate sovereign nations who were now in the process of being forcibly integrated into American society. The Native liberation movement wasn't about claiming an "Indian place" in white society; it was about maintaining the separateness of Native society. "What the different racial and minority groups had needed," writes Deloria, "was not a new legal device for obliterating differences, but mutual respect with economic and political independence."

With the exception of the nationalist Black Power movement, the civil rights struggle had little relevance to Native struggles. The Black Power movement, from the point of view of Native militants, talked about many of the same things—sovereignty, self-organization, self-determination—but lacked the one crucial element that the Native nations already possessed; a land base. While African-Americans formed a majority in many US cities, they nowhere possessed a land base sufficient for a sovereign national existence. Further, to produce the common cultural ties which were necessary for a nationalist movement, the Black Power advocates had to look to a nonexistent idealized "African" culture (in essence, melding together elements from a number of diverse African cultures), and lacked a native culture of their own.

For these reasons, the Native militants concluded, the Black Nationalist movement died out, and the Black liberation struggle returned to its goal of integration and the acceptance of African-Americans into mainstream culture. The Native American struggles, by contrast, center around a pre-existing cultural tradition and land base, and have been from the beginning movements of true national liberation.

Most white radicals have failed to make the distinction. For the most part, Marxists and Leninists have tended to view traditionalist societies such as the Native American nations, the Ainu of the Japanese Islands, the Rama and Miskito of eastern Nicaragua, the Bahnar "Montagnards" of Vietnam, the Kurds of Iran and Iraq, the !Kung of southern Africa, or the Yanomamo and Jivaro of the Amazon Basin, as side issues. Marxist theory, when it treats these traditional societies at all, treats them as backward anachronisms which never "developed", and who thus have fallen inevitably to capitalist domination and exploitation. Despite the fact that the historical, cultural and economic circumstances of these native societies are unique, Marxists have tended to lump them together with the rest of the "victims of imperialist exploitation" — the neo-colonies, women, African-Americans and Latinos.

Native activists, for their part, have long been openly critical of the Marxian outlook, particularly its Leninist incarnation. Native traditionalists have had few kind words to say about Marxists, and the Leninists have in turn viewed Native traditionalists as reactionaries or worse.

Marx's work was largely limited to that of studying and explaining the history and social development of capitalism in the European nations. However, he did at various times comment briefly on the capitalists' treatment of "primitive peoples", and his attitude accurately reflected the Victorian era in which he lived. Marx held that the "barbaric races" should be civilized, turned into workers and proletarians, and from there fight for the overthrow of capitalism.

For instance, in 1853, Marx, the "father of internationalism", praised the British conquest and occupation of India, saying that it helped to civilize and industrialize the natives and thus prepare them for socialism: "England has to fulfill a double mission in India, one destructive, the other regenerating; the annihilation of old Asiatic society, and the laying of the material foundation of western society in Asia." In a similar vein, Engels wrote, "The conquest of Algeria is an important and fortunate fact for the progress of civilization."

This Euro-centric attitude, which assumes that European culture and economic structures are inherently superior to those of the "primitive" world, logically produces the racist notion that the task of the European nations is to "civilize the savages". In order to thus "take up the white man's burden", North Americans waged bloody wars which devastated entire Native nations, herded the survivors onto desolate reservations, banned their tribal customs and religions, suppressed their native languages, and kidnapped their children and sent them to far-away "boarding schools", where they were forcibly indoctrinated into Anglo language and culture.

Marx, while condemning the brutality of this colonial process, nevertheless remained convinced that it was beneficial in the long run, since it introduced social structures and economic changes that laid the foundation for a socialist economy. Lenin, in turn, accepted the proposition that the penetration of non-capitalist areas by imperialism was progressive.

Ever since, Marxist-Leninists have continued to reinforce this attitude with their casual use of Euro-centric terms such as "primitive society", "pre-capitalist economic formations", and "undeveloped nations". By using these terms to refer to traditionalist societies, Marxist-Leninists are revealing an unspoken conviction that these societies are "inferior" to the industrialized capitalist nations, and that the best thing they can do is to become "developed", to "catch up" and thus "advance" towards socialism. As American Indian Movement leader Russell Means puts it, "Marx himself calls us 'pre-capitalist' and 'primitive'. Pre-capitalist simply means that, in his view, we would eventually discover capitalism and become capitalists; we have always been economically retarded in Marxist terms."

Some may object that Marx was merely describing an already existing state of affairs or an ongoing process when he observed that Britain was "civilizing" India. Capitalism, Marx pointed out, was inherently expansionistic and must constantly seek out new markets if it is to survive. It is one thing, however, to assert that capitalism will encroach whenever possible upon traditionalist non-capitalist areas; it is quite another thing to assert that it is beneficial to do so.

On the whole, however, Marxism and Leninism have simply remained irrelevant to native peoples. Socialists have likewise tended to ignore native issues unless these issues allowed them to "radicalize" and recruit people. The American Left, points out Native American activist Ward Churchill, seems to have taken the position that "to be preoccupied with Native American issues, one has to be a Native. . . Non-Indians simply have more important things to think about."

American radicals virtually ignored the militant Native American movement for much of its history. When the "Tribes of All Nations" occupied Alcatraz Island in 1970, few Leftists even noticed. Even the occupation of the Bureau of Indian Affairs building in Washington DC, during the "Trail of Broken Treaties", produced no debate within the Left. It was not until the American Indian Movement occupied the village of Wounded Knee in February 1973 that the Left "noticed" Native struggles. During Wounded Knee II, a steady stream of radicals made the pilgrimage to South Dakota, stood in front of the TV cameras and microphones, and solemnly declared their solidarity with the oppressed Native peoples.

Furthermore, in their revolutionary practice, Marxist-Leninists in the Soviet Union, Vietnam and Nicaragua have demonstrated no greater sympathy towards Native traditions and cultures than have the monopoly capitalists. The Soviet Union, in its program of "Russification", crushed ethnic and national movements in Georgia, the Ukraine and the Central Asian Soviet Republics, forcing native people to accept Russian political and cultural hegemony. The Vietnamese have viciously attacked the Bahnar tribes of the central mountains, while the Sandinistas took it upon themselves to "relocate" the Rama, Miskito and Sumo tribes of Nicaragua's Atlantic coast. Native activists may perhaps be forgiven for comparing the monstrosities the Leninists have inflicted upon them with the brutality of the capitalists and declaring that they cannot see the difference between them.

Many Native activists have declared that they consider their enemy to be, not the capitalist economic structure in particular, but the blind process of industrialization which accompanies it. The inherent needs of an industrialized and mechanized economy, these activists assert, drive it to pillage the earth, to spew poisons into the air and water, to destroy the land in their search for new raw materials, and to ignore the environmental impact of their actions in a mad quest for an ever-increasing ability to produce things.

The Marxist-Leninist nations, moreover, accept and embrace this rationale of increased industrialization, and, if anything, this drive is even stronger in them because of the need to "catch up" with the industrialized West. The Leninists are thus driven in the same manner to occupy Native lands and to pillage the earth to feed their own industrial machine, all the while creating ecological and environmental catastrophes of their own. "I see," says Russell Means, "that the territory of the USSR used to contain a number of tribal peoples, and that they have been crushed to make way for the factories."

Thus, many Native activists have concluded, Marxism-Leninism is nothing more than a mirror image of the old capitalist emphasis on wealth, production and material gain, with no regard for the human costs. Means concludes:

> Revolutionary Marxism is committed to even further perfection of the very industrial process which is destroying us all. It is offering only to "redistribute" the results, the money maybe, of this industrialization to a wider section of the population. . . It's the same old song, but maybe with a faster tempo this time.

Some Marxist-Leninists may answer that it is not the industrial process per se which produces environmental degradation, but rather the blind commercial social framework within which it is utilized. It is undoubtedly true that a socialist society will seek to place its resources where they will do the most good — it will place industry at the service of humanity rather than the other way around. And undoubtedly the structure and components of the industrial process will be altered in an environmentally safe manner; the use of solar and other renewable sources of energy, mass transport rather than inefficient automobiles, etc.

By itself, however, this will not be enough. Socialism must bring about a profound change in the manner in which humanity relates itself to its surroundings. Marxists, the Native activists say, must throw off once and for all the capitalist notion of Nature as something to be conquered and utilized by humanity. Instead, as both radical environmentalists and Native activists point out, we must embrace an outlook which recognizes the essential unity between humanity and the natural process — a naturalistic outlook which understands and maintains the constant interpenetration between humanity and its environment.

Such an outlook can be found in Marx — in the Marx of the 1844 *Economic and Philosophic Manuscripts*, who wrote: "Nature is man's inorganic body. . . Man lives within Nature, with which he must remain in constant intercourse if he is not to die." These naturalist words could well have been spoken by any Lakota *wichasha wakan*. The Lakota refer to this interrelationship as *mitakuye oyasin*, "all of my relationships".

Thus, instead of merely focusing on a process of industrial expansion to enable the neo-colonies to "catch up" with the industrialized capitalists, Marxists must begin to focus more on the effects of industrialization, and one of the most fundamental of these revolves around the relationship between our industrial technology and our natural surroundings. Native activists declare that we must give up our obsession of obtaining for everyone the same high "standard of living" found in the industrial nations, and must realize that these were obtained at enormous and unacceptable costs. Too many Marxists, they say, share the old advertising slogan of the DuPont Chemical Company—"Better living through chemicals".

If socialism is to be relevant to the Native activists, then Marxists must be concerned with the process of de-industrialization rather than with the higher expansion of productive forces; of dismantling capitalist industries which are wasteful, dangerous and environmentally unsound. Marx remarked that British colonialism was beneficial because it raised the Indian people's material well-being and thus prepared them for socialism. But we cannot be said to be helping a people when we export nuclear waste to them and strip-mine for coal on their lands. When we spray toxic chemicals onto their food and sell them unsafe products, we cannot say that we are helping them prepare the material base for socialism. The exploitation of Native peoples, by Marxist-Leninists as well as capitalists, must be vigorously opposed.

Marx, however, was writing at a time when the industrial process was still in its teens. Furthermore, Marx never expected that the capitalist system would live long enough to greatly expand this industrial system; he believed it would fall upon a transitional "socialist state" to complete this process and thus provide the material abundance necessary for a communist economy. Marx was never able to see the phenomenal expansion of productive capability under monopoly capitalism, and thus never saw the devastating effects these have had. On these questions, Marxists have much to learn from the Native activists.

Instead, however, most Marxists have castigated Native activists as "back-to-nature freaks" who, like the Luddites, refuse to accept the inevitable, and who instead long for a return to a non-existent idyllic pastoral life.

This unfair distortion hides the profound message within Native criticism. Whatever befalls the earth befalls the children of the earth, under a communist system no less than under a capitalist one. Asserting that society must reject continuous industrial development does not mean that we all have to live in caves, hunt deer or buffalo, or eat berries and roots. Native activists do not advocate a "return to nature"; rather, they serve to remind us that we can never *leave* Nature, that we are a part of it and can exist only through constant intercourse with it.

Alienated capitalist and Leninist ideology, which both seek to "make Man the master of Nature", have lost sight of humanity's fundamental interrelationship with our natural surroundings, and therefore have encouraged us to run roughshod over it. Traditional activists have not lost sight of this, and can do much to help us regain it.

A major reason why this relationship has been ignored by most Marxists is that, in the course of its development, the ideology of Marxism-Leninism has lost its most salient feature — its emphasis on the dialectics of development. The emphasis on relational dialectics is the linchpin of Marxism.

Humans, Marx pointed out, must make their living through labor, through the process of extracting and modifying natural materials. To do this effectively, humans must form social frameworks which allow them to extract the necessities of life from their natural surroundings, and distribute these to the members of the social group.

By thus acting upon their natural surroundings, humans are at the same time modifying them through their actions. These changes in natural surroundings produce changes in those human organizations which relate to them, and thus, through an interconnecting dialectical process, alters human social structures. In essence, human actions produce changes in material surroundings, which in turn necessitate new changes in human actions.

When these changes in material surroundings become great enough, the old framework of human social structures which grew within them are no longer suited for them, and humans cannot efficiently obtain their necessities of life. Thus, an entirely new system of social structure must be formed in order to interact efficiently with these new material surroundings. When population and environmental pressures forced humans to move from gathering wild plants for food to deliberately cultivating food crops, for instance, an entirely new relationship was produced between humanity and its natural surroundings. The old "hunter-gatherer" mode of social structure could not cope with this reality, and was forced to give way to a new "feudalist" structure, based upon agriculture.

This dialectical relationship, Marx concluded, is the key to understanding human social development. Humans are forced by their surroundings to organize in certain ways to obtain their means of life, but in so organizing they influence and alter those surroundings. When the old method of organization is no longer suited to these changing circumstances, it falls and is replaced by a more efficient form of social organization. In this manner, this interrelationship between humanity and its surroundings produces the constant process of social change which we call history.

Unfortunately, Marx's profound insight quickly fell victim to the capitalist paradigm within which it had developed. At the time Marx formulated his views, the capitalist ideologists had become enamored with the "positive sciences", which viewed the natural process as being objective and independent of human activity. This notion fit in well with the capitalist goal of "conquering Nature" and utilizing it in the process of production.

Beginning with Engels, Marx's dialectical approach underwent modification, until it had been transformed into a positive science, akin to the natural sciences of biology or physics. Human society, these "economic determinists" asserted, developed according to eternal and unchanging "laws of human development", and these natural laws were as regular and predictable as those which governed the motions of the planets or the behavior of atoms.

This "positivist" view reached its pinnacle with the Leninists, who asserted that they could understand and interpret these laws, and thus could lead human society to conformity with the requirements of its "scientific development". Thus, Stalin and the other Leninists have been able to justify their oppression, exploitation and elimination of national and ethnic peoples in the name of the "objective scientific development of history".

Similar assertions have been made by modern Marxist-Leninists concerning the Native tribes. For the most part, the Leninist attitude towards the Native peoples is that, while what is happening to them is sad and tragic, they are the unfortunate victims of the "laws of development" which, they say, demands the destruction of "primitive society" on its way to socialism.

This idea of "law of development" is closely allied with the Marxist theory of "stages of history". According to this view, all human societies develop in a regular and predictable way as their economic structures change and produce new social superstructures. "In broad outline," Marx writes, "we can designate the Asiatic, the ancient, the feudal and the modern bourgeois modes of production as so many epochs in the progress of the economic formation of society."

The tribal societies fall into what Marx would refer to as the "Asiatic mode of production", which, according to the Marxist-Leninists, is characterized by a stagnant, unprogressive system of communal lands or villages. According to the tenets of the laws of development, these primitive societies would inevitably transform themselves into "ancient modes of production", characterized by slave labor, and thence to feudal agrarian societies. The feudal mode in turn fell to capitalism, which would, sometime in the future, be inevitably forced to give way to socialism. This pattern, the Leninists assert, would be followed by humans everywhere, thus leading to the inevitable destruction of tribal and other "primitive" societies.

Native activists, understandably, have been reluctant to relinquish their tribal culture and identity in the name of "the inevitable". While it may or not be a tendency for capitalism and state socialism to attempt to overwhelm and eliminate the traditional cultures, there is certainly no natural tendency for native nations to give up without a fight.

By expounding their notion of "natural law", the Marxists have once again demonstrated the Euro-centrism of their thinking. Marxism developed from a study of capitalism, and capitalism has only developed in the Anglo-European countries. The "positivist" outlook of Marxism-Leninism asserts as a matter of course that the rest of the world can only slavishly follow the same "natural laws" which produced the capitalist Anglo-European nations. Social progress, in this view, consists in moving steadily along this path from primitive communalism to feudalism to capitalism to socialism.

Marx himself, however, criticized this "positivist" interpretation. His work, he pointed out, was a "historical sketch of the genesis of capitalism in Western Europe", not a "historical-philosophic theory of a general path every people is fated to tread." Marx concluded that the social history of other regions of the world was apt to differ sharply from that of Europe. He wrote:

> Events strikingly analogous but taking place in different historical surroundings led to totally different results. By studying each of these forms of evolution separately and then comparing them, one can easily find the clue to this phenomenon, but one will never arrive there by using as one's master key a general historical-philosophical theory, the supreme virtue of which consists in its being super-historical."

Human development, according to Marx's thought, develops in tandem with material conditions. If these material conditions are different, however, it does not necessarily follow that the course of human development will be everywhere the same, or that all nations are fated to follow the path taken by the "advanced" Anglo-European nations. The fact that Native American nations never "developed" into feudalism or capitalism is not due to the fact that they are "primitive" or "backwards"; rather, the simple fact is that these nations didn't change because there was never any reason for them to do so.

In the traditional societies, therefore, the so-called "stages of history" were never needed. Traditional peoples exist in communalist societies which are very similar to those envisioned by the socialists. In fact, Marx himself remarked on occasion that socialism did nothing more than reproduce the classless society which he called "primitive communism", but reproduced it at a much higher level of economic ability.

Thus, the possibility remained open for such societies to avoid the necessity of a feudalist or capitalist "stage". For this to happen, a highly efficient means of producing the necessities of life for this society must exist, thus avoiding the class distinctions which arise from scarcity. As an example, Marx cited the traditional Russian *mir*, a village commune which, he thought, could provide the basis for a socialist society if a revolution in Europe freed that continent's economic resources and made them available for everyone.

By applying this principle to our current circumstances, we can see that the Native nations lack only the economic capacity which would allow them to communally share abundant wealth and lift them from material poverty and want. They do not need a new structure for their society, nor do they need to be "civilized" or "developed". The culture they have had for centuries — no standing army, no authoritarian government, no possessing class, communal production, all decisions by consensus, distribution according to need — has served them admirably well and has much to teach the industrialized nations about how a socialist society is to be run.

What the Native nations need most of all is to be left alone, to be allowed to live as they have for centuries — as independent, sovereign nations. They do not need the "Marxist-Leninists" to come in and tell them what they should or shouldn't be doing. They do not need to be "radicalized" or brought into the "larger struggle".

If the socialists want to do anything useful for the Native American nations, they should seize the incredible productive capacity and wealth of the United States (which after all had been originally seized from the Native nations) and make it available without restrictions, allowing the Native nations to use what they need in whatever manner they want. This will happen only after the industrialized Anglo-European nations have at last "caught up" to the Native nations, and return to a social structure which re- establishes the natural relationships between humans and their surroundings without causing harm to either.

Unfortunately, Marxist-Leninist statements about what will happen to the indigenous American peoples "after the revolution" are not very encouraging. The Revolutionary Communist Party has this to say:

> This will most definitely not be a new chapter in the history of oppression of Indian peoples — forcing them onto reservations and treating them like special "wards of the state". Indeed, the new proletarian state, while favoring and encouraging unity and integration, will insure these formerly oppressed peoples' right to autonomy as part of the policy of promoting real equality between nations and peoples.
>
> The proletariat will, through consultation with the masses of Indian peoples, establish large areas of land where they can live and work, and will provide special assistance to the Indian peoples in developing these areas. Here autonomy will be the policy of the proletarian state — the various Indian peoples will have the right to self-government within the larger socialist state, under certain overall guiding principles.
>
> The proletariat will encourage and support the development of separate national forms of culture, all serving the proletarian revolution in their content. . . Only far in the future, when communism has been achieved, including through the struggle for national equality, will nations be superseded and will the national differences, including in the areas of cultures, be transcended.

This program, of "autonomy within the larger state", of "unity and integration", of "transcendence of national differences", would sound familiar to most Native activists. They would know that there is another word for this — "assimilation" — and it means nothing more than the acceptance of the Anglo-European's culture by everyone else. Another word for it would be "cultural genocide".

It is no wonder that most Native American activists reject the Leninists' proposed "workers' paradise". The Native nations have no intention of submerging their national and cultural identity into the "larger state", nor are they willing to modify their traditional cultures to "serve the proletarian revolution". As Lakota activist Frank Black Elk declares, "The only social order I have the least bit of interest in joining is an independent Lakota Nation."

It should be clear that Native nations will never achieve national independence within the existing socio-political structure of the industrial nations. Native people may wish that the whites would just go away or disappear, but they won't. Natives may beg the whites to give them back their land and their national sovereignty, but they won't. Natives may ask the corporations to stop the economic and environmental exploitation of Native lands, but they won't. Only a radical change in the social relationships of white society — a revolution — can stop these abuses.

What sort of revolution do the Native peoples need? First, they must be able to seize control of their own destiny, to maintain their own cultural identities and their own national sovereignty. In the United States, this means deposing the IRA-imposed puppet tribal governments and returning to true self-government and sovereign self-organization. As Ward Churchill puts it:

> No human solution to the overall issues confronting any American radical can reasonably be said to exist, should it exclude mechanisms through which to safeguard the residual land base and cultural identities of these people.
>
> Unless the Left acknowledges this, there is potentially no difference between the Left and the Right in their impact on the Native Americans. On the face of it, matters will be essentially the same; the Indians will be divested of control over their last remaining resources by all factions of the Euro-American political spectrum, unless the Left can articulate a coherent formulation of priorities and values allowing for (at the very least) maintenance of the Indian/white status quo in terms of land base.

"The alternative to a satisfactory solution in this instance," Churchill concludes, "is genocide."

The Native nations, if they are to have real sovereignty and independence, must be able to seize control of the economic resources which still exist in their land area, and they must have control of enough economic resources to support themselves. Current Native lands hold some two-thirds of all readily-extractable energy resources in the United States, a resource which, if brought under the direct control of the Native American nations, would provide an important economic base. If all treaties with the United States would be enforced, Native tribes would control some one-third of the continental US, enough to allow these sovereign nations to become economically and politically independent.

Such sovereign independence is, however, dependent upon Native control of their own resources — upon national liberation. As a resolution adopted at the 1980 Black Hill International Survival Gathering declares:

> When control of the use of land is held by the people who live on it, technology will be in the control of the people. This is a keystone to all of our survival.

Such a national liberation cannot happen by itself, however. Because native Americans are not strong enough, politically or militarily, to free themselves from white domination, the Native nations will not gain real sovereignty and independence until the social institutions of the industrialized nations are broken, until the economic resources that were seized by the ruling elites are expropriated and placed at the disposal of human society. This is the role that Marxian socialists must play to help the Native nations in their struggle for independence.

Environmentalism

We have already seen that ecological concerns form a large part of the basis for Native American demands for self-determination. In many respects, the concerns of the Native activists have been re-iterated and expanded by the radical environmentalists.

Marx and Engels had little to say about environmentalism or the impact of industrial development upon natural systems. They shared the Victorian belief that industry was humanity's crowning achievement, and that the scientific application of technology could solve any human problem.

Nevertheless, both Marx and Engels pointed to examples of environmental degradation caused by capitalism's industrial machinery. Engels, in *The Condition of the Working Class in England*, pointed out:

> The air of London is neither so pure nor so rich in oxygen as that of the countryside; two and a half million pairs of lungs and 250,000 coal fires concentrated in an area of three to four geographical square miles use up an immense amount of oxygen, which can only be replaced with difficulty. . . River water is so dirty as to be useless for cleaning purposes.

Marx noted that "every advance in capitalist agriculture is an advance in the art, not only of robbing the workers, but also of robbing the soil," leading to the "ruin of the permanent sources of this fertility":

> Capitalist production, therefore, only develops the techniques and organization of the social process of production by simultaneously undermining the sources of all wealth; land and the workers.

Under socialism, Marx wrote, people would need to be "rationally regulating their exchange with nature . . . with the least expenditure of energy and under conditions most worthy of their human nature."

Marx also concluded that humans had an obligation to leave a viable environment to future generations:

> From the standpoint of a higher socio-economic formation, individual private ownership of the earth will appear just as much in bad taste as the ownership of one human being by another. Even a whole society, a nation or all contemporary societies taken together, are not the absolute owners of the earth. They are only its occupants, its beneficiaries, and like a good paterfamilias must leave it in an improved condition to future generations.

For the most part, Marx's comments concerning what would today be called "environmental issues" took place within a debate over the ideas of Thomas Robert Malthus. In 1798, Malthus had written a booklet entitled *Essay on the Principle of Population*, which argued the thesis that, since the population of a country grows exponentially and the production of food grows only linearly, population would inevitably outrun food production, leading to widespread famine and starvation.

The only method of preventing this dilemma, Malthus concluded, was to remove the "excess" portion of the population. Since, in his view, humans were "inert, sluggish and averse from labor, unless compelled by necessity," it is no surprise that Malthus declared the industrious property owners to be valuable, and the indigent poor to be "excess". Malthus thus openly encouraged steps which would lead to the physical elimination of poor people. He called for the repeal of the Poor Laws, which provided charity and relief to unemployed families, hoping thus to allow the poor to die off and reduce the population. Marx, for his part, referred to Malthus as a "baboon" and a "lackey for the bourgeoisie".

In the early 1970's, various "ecology" groups were formed to fight the pollution of the environment. Many of these environmentalists soon took to preaching a new version of Malthus's thesis of overpopulation.

Perhaps the best-known of these "neo-Malthusians" was Paul Ehrlich, who, in 1968, wrote *The Population Bomb*. Ehrlich updated Malthus by arguing that not only food production tended to fall behind as population levels increased, but that overpopulation produced a drain on all other human resources — energy supplies and other products. Ehrlich asserted that environmental degradation could only be halted by a policy of "zero population growth":

> Too many cars, too many factories, too much detergent, too much pesticide, multiplying contrails, inadequate sewage treatment plants, too little water, too much carbon dioxide — all can be traced easily to too many people.

The answer to the problem, as Ehrlich saw it, was to take steps to reduce the population. And, it quickly became apparent, the neo-Malthusians had definite ideas about whose population ought to be reduced. Ehrlich called for a policy of giving economic aid only to those nations which took steps to control their populations and which had the possibility of becoming "food self-sufficient". Rich nations which did not need economic aid, of course, could continue to do as they pleased; poorer nations would starve.

This idea became known as "triage", after the practice of medical technicians who, after a disaster, separate the victims into three groups — those who will survive without treatment, those who will die even if treated, and those who can be saved with immediate treatment — and then treating only the latter. Under this plan, as writer Richard Rubenstein puts it:

> Famine-stricken nations are divided into three basic categories; those capable of returning to work if given first-aid supplies, those that would become food-viable and rehabilitate their economies with foreign assistance, and those incapable of rehabilitation even with massive foreign aid. The last group are to be written off entirely.

In 1974, psychologist Garrett Hardin was even more explicit when he wrote an essay entitled *Lifeboat Ethics: The Case Against Helping the Poor*. The policies advocated by this paper were virtually identical with those of Malthus when he fought against the Poor Laws. Among other things, Hardin advocated that the government release a set number of "reproduction licenses", which would allow only a certain number of children to be born every year. Rich people, of course, would be able to purchase as many licenses as they wished, while poor people would be thus prevented from reproducing. The plan also called for government actions to limit the number of females in society (and thus the number of births). In this neo-fascistic scheme, the "worthy" would survive, while the "inferior" would die.

The most militant of these new environmental groups was Earth First!, which rose to prominence in the 1980's with a bumper sticker that flatly declared, "Malthus was right!" Like the rest of the neo-Malthusians, Earth First! calls for "the reduction of the human population to an ecologically sustainable level." Unlike Malthus, however, who was content to merely remove poor people from the earth in order to ease overpopulation, Earth First! often sounds as though it wants to remove *everybody*. Earth First! supporter Christopher Manes refers to humanity as a "relatively expendable part" of the environment, while EF! co-founder David Foreman calls himself and his group "antibodies against the human pox that's ravaging this precious beautiful planet".

In 1987, Foreman wrote an article suggesting that the wave of famines in Africa was beneficial to the environment because it helped to remove excess people:

> The worst thing we could do in Ethiopia is to give aid – the best thing would be to just let nature seek its own balance, to let the people there just starve.

Another Earth First! article declared that the worldwide AIDS epidemic was also beneficial: "If radical environmentalists were to invent a disease to bring human population back to ecological sanity, it would probably be something like AIDS."

Other EF! activists have called, perhaps tongue in cheek, for the Defense Department to develop a biological weapon that would only be lethal to humans, so that, when the next war comes and we wipe ourselves out, at least the rest of the ecosphere won't be affected. One Earth First!er once told me that he didn't believe the world would ever get better until there were no longer any people on it. He refused my offer to drive him to the nearest bridge so he could jump off, thus helping to ease our overpopulation problem.

Earth First! declares that the planet is in a state of "biological meltdown", an increasing destruction of the ecological balance and the elimination of countless other species, all brought about by the actions of human society. As Manes puts it:

> The biological meltdown is most directly the result of values fundamental to what we have come to recognize as culture under the regime of technological society; economic growth, "progress", property rights, consumerism, religious doctrines about humanity's dominion over nature, technocratic notions about achieving an optimum human existence at the expense of all other life-forms.

"To talk about the environmental crisis in its modern context," Manes concludes, "is to talk about the role of technology in human affairs."

For this reason, Earth First! declares that it is fighting against technological society and also against "that part of it powerful and affluent enough to hold the reins of technological innovation." Says Manes:

> Nobody asked society at large if it wanted nuclear power, or DDT or asbestos insulation. Government agencies and multinational corporations make most of the decisions about what technologies are introduced into society.

The tactics used by Earth First! in its anti-technology fight center around "ecotage", or the use of nonviolent sabotage to cripple industrial machinery, delay anti-environmental operations such as logging, and attack government and corporate offices which promote anti-ecological activities. Using the tactics of "monkeywrenching", EF! members have fought the "industrial monster" by driving steel spikes into trees to discourage logging, by disabling bulldozers and other logging equipment, and by sabotaging roads which lead into wilderness areas.

Despite their open and militant opposition to the corporations, Earth First! specifically declares that it is not interested in politics. The organization, Foreman (a former Marine) declares, "does not aim to overthrow any social, political or economic system. Even Republicans can monkeywrench."

In fact, Earth First!'s solution to environmental problems is much more extreme than a mere change in social structures — they want to *do away* with most social structures. "The problem," says Manes, "goes deeper than the monolithic and destructive technologies of civilization. Civilization itself seems to be the problem."

Thus, Earth First! advocates that humans return to a "pre-industrial" social order — "Back to the Pleistocene!" The EF! publishing company is named Ned Ludd Books, after the British Luddite leader who smashed machinery in order to prevent the introduction of the Industrial Revolution.

The Earth First! models of ecologically-sound society are "those cultures that have developed a sustainable and harmonious relationship with their surroundings, because they neither industrialized nor turned to monoculture. . . Out of some hidden source of wisdom, these societies chose not to dominate nature." Among the "ecologically wise" societies cited by Earth First! are the Penan tribes of Malaysia, the Piromasco Indians of the Peruvian Amazon, and the !Kung "Bushmen" hunter/gatherers of the Kalahari Desert in Africa.

Not all modern environmentalists, however, accept the apocalyptic outlook of the neo-Malthusians (ecologist Brian Tokar has called Earth First! "outrightly hostile to the human race"). Instead of looking to the pressures of an excess population to explain environmental decay, many researchers are focusing on the social structures of society, on the ways in which society extracts, manufactures and distributes wealth. Rather than simply blaming pollution on too many poor people, as do the neo-Malthusians, these researchers blame the social relations which produce so many poor people.

One of the leaders in this field has been Barry Commoner, the Director of the Center for the Biology of Natural Systems in New York. "The chief reason for the environmental crisis that has engulfed the United States in recent years," Commoner writes, "is the sweeping transformation of productive technology since World War II." In the last fifty years, Commoner asserts, the actual amount of economic goods produced for every person in the country has not changed significantly. "What has changed drastically," he notes, "is the technology of production, rather than over-all output of the economic good":

> Soap powder has been displaced by synthetic detergents, natural fibers (cotton and wool) have been displaced by synthetic ones, steel and lumber have been displaced by aluminum, plastic and concrete, railroad freight has been displaced by truck freight, returnable bottles have been displaced by nonreturnable ones.

In each of these instances, Commoner points out, a common product was replaced by a similar product, but one that had a greatly expanded impact upon ecological systems. He lays the blame for this process at the feet of the industrial corporate giants—the new environmentally-unsound products, while not any better than the old ecologically-safer ones, were much more profitable.

Rather than advocating that poor people die off and that the rest of us live in caves and eat roots, these environmentalists advocate deep changes in the economic and industrial structures currently practiced by the wealthy nations. "Ecological survival," says Commoner, "does not mean the abandonment of technology. Rather, it requires that technology be derived from a scientific analysis that is appropriate to the natural world on which technology intrudes."

The neo-Malthusians scoff at this, saying that more technology will only increase the problem. Christopher Manes writes:

> Perhaps a technology that includes the interests of both the human and ecological communities is possible, but one suspects it would look very much like the crafts that primal people pursue, and not the high-tech dreams of the anti-environmentalists.

Already, however, a number of trends can be seen in bourgeois society that point to drastic changes in technological and economic structures—changes which are becoming technologically as well as environmentally necessary (the problem of global warming is quickly becoming one of the most important prods for new technological and social changes).

The electric industry is a case in point. Modern coal- or oil-fired electric power plants are huge technological monsters that spew out a variety of ecological poisons, and contribute to such global dangers as acid rain and global warming. Each of these expensive plants is built in a central area, with the resulting electricity carried to users in the surrounding area through transmission wires and towers.

This method of transmission, however, is grossly inefficient — it costs a great deal, and a large portion of the electric power which is produced is absorbed by the transmission system and lost. These problems have led some in the electric industry to view the central power station as a wasteful and out-moded piece of equipment.

The solution to the problems of centrally-generated electricity may lie in the area of solar energy. The production of power and electricity is always more efficient when it is carried out at the point of use — a strategy that cannot be followed by large coal-fired plants. If current research fulfills its promise, however, solar energy will be able to easily and cheaply produce electricity using solar panels which are mounted on the same building in which the resulting power is to be used. By using solar panels, the expensive and environmentally-damaging central power stations can be replaced by cheap, limitless and efficient energy at the point of use.

Another major source of environmental pollution can be traced to modern farming methods. Large farms, increasingly owned and operated by large corporate "agribusiness" firms, attempt to increase their yield per acre (and thus their profitability) by spraying huge amounts of chemical fertilizers, insecticides, fungicides and weed-killers. All of these toxic chemicals find their way into the food chain, where they are concentrated and can reach lethal levels.

In some areas, however, experiments have been carried out using decentralized "organic farming" methods. In this technique, a large number of fields are worked with natural fertilizers and biological pest controls, without the use of artificial chemicals. Studies have shown that the yield per acre from these farms is nearly the same (about 85%)of the yield from conventional farms, at a greatly reduced environmental impact. Further, organic farms have been designed which utilize their own waste vegetable products to produce ethanol for use as fuel in farm machinery, thus reducing the use of non-renewable fossil fuels.

Another major polluter in industrial society is the internal combustion automobile engine. As gasoline prices have been driven higher and higher, automobile manufacturers have finally responded with smaller, lighter cars that use less fuel and produce fewer noxious exhaust gases such as nitrous oxide and lead. Researchers have not yet put much effort, however, into a less-profitable but more-practical electric automobile engine that would use no fossil fuel and produce no harmful exhausts.

Unlike the neo-Malthusians, the "neo-Marxist" environmentalists have no wish to reduce people to a Stone Age standard of living. Rather, says Canadian writer Robert Paehlke, "The future success of environmentalism depends on a reasonable level of security for the majority in society." Many ecologists, moreover, have begun to question whether continued economic growth and industrial expansion is really needed to provide everybody with a comfortable standard of living.

The business elite, of course, has long argued that any environmentalist restrictions which hamper the continued growth of the economy will produce a falling standard of living for everybody. In essence, the "progressive" business community has argued for a "green capitalism", in which the technological methods and industrial techniques are changed, but the basic economic structure remains the same. This, of course, would insure that the elite would continue to have a high standard of living, while the rest, unless there was a simultaneous re-distribution of wealth, would continue in relative poverty.

On the other hand, some ecologists have argued that, in order to reduce environmental degradation, "all of us" have to reduce our standard of living and ease the strain on the planet. As biologist Wayne Davis puts it, "Blessed be the starving Blacks of Mississippi, with their outdoor privies, for they are ecologically sound, and they shall inherit a nation."

Not much of a nation, though. This ethic, often summarized in the slogan "Live simply, that others may simply live," is most often preached by those who are already economically well-off. Poor people in impoverished areas, needless to say, are less anxious to settle for less in order to be "ecological".

Other environmentalists have already pointed out that our planet already has more than enough economic resources to provide for everyone without expanding our productive output to ecologically unsafe levels. In 1970, the US Commission on Economic Growth and the American Future concluded, in a much-ignored report:

> There is little question that the United States has the resources, if it chooses to use them, to meet the demands of a population growing at the current rate as well as to correct various social and economic inequalities.

The basic problem, the neo-Marxist environmentalists conclude, isn't that there isn't enough food to go around; the problem is that those who need food are desperately poor, and no one will give them food unless they can pay for it. As the French Marxist Andre Gorz puts it:

> Nothing — other than the logic of capitalism — prevents us from manufacturing and making available to everyone adequate accommodation, clothing, household equipment, and forms of transportation which are energy-conserving, simple to repair, and long-lasting, while simultaneously increasing the amount of free time and the amount of truly useful products available to the population.

The problem is not that we are not able to produce sufficient resources for so many people; the problem is that those resources which are produced are monopolized by a small segment of the population, with little or none going to the rest.

Thus, unlike the neo-Malthusian Earth First! (which says "We need not worry about how to restructure society in order to accommodate our proposals [because] we're not in the business of trying to save civilization"), the neo- Marxist environmentalists realize that environmental degradation can only be reversed if drastic changes are made in our technical and social structures. As ecologist David Dickson notes:

> Only by realizing the extent to which technology provides an integral part of the ideology of contemporary society, at the same time as forming an essential element of the mechanism by which the supremacy of existing political systems are maintained, can we see the extent to which the need to develop an alternative technology is both necessary and desirable.

Such an alternative industrial structure is impossible to achieve within bourgeois society. The capitalist elite has fought viciously against any meaningful environmental reforms, labeling them a "regulatory burden" on businesses.

It is no surprise that the bourgeoisie should view radical environmentalism as such a severe threat. Ecological criticisms of modern technology and industrial processes are a direct challenge to the economic structures which allow the bourgeoisie to maintain its position of power and privilege. An attack on technological decisions is also a direct attack on the industrial capitalists who make these decisions, challenging its economic authority and its hold on industrial decision-making power. These strike at the very heart of capitalist power.

Most corporate giants deny that they are even responsible for pollution or environmental damage. When Sherman Knapp, the Chairman of Northeast Utilities, was asked what causes pollution, he replied, "It is not industry per se, but the demands of the public. . . If we can convince the national and local leaders in the environmental crusade of this basic logic, then we can help them focus their attention on the major aspect of the problem." Thus, in a perverse echo of the neo-Malthusian view, the corporate polluters assert that it is the excess people in the world, and not environmentally-unsound corporate practices, which have to disappear.

It is clear that the industrial and technological changes called for by the radical environmentalists cannot be made within a capitalist framework. Under a market system, the owners of capital seek a return on their investment, and their investment is the money they lay out for capital — materials, labor, equipment. By virtue of the structure of the free-market economy, the capitalist is able to ignore the other, hidden costs of his technological decisions — the costs of toxic waste cleanup, of refuse disposal, of repairing environmental damage — that the owners of capital do not have to directly pay. In other words, these hidden costs are "externalized" and "socialized"; they are not figured into the profit and loss statements of the polluting industries, but are instead paid by everybody else.

"What is needed," says Commoner, "is a kind of 'ecological impact inventory' for each productive activity, which will enable us to attach a sort of pollution price tag to each product." The structure of capitalism, however, insures that no such accounting will ever be made. The system of private ownership of industry and private technological decision-making is simply unable to take social costs into consideration. Such an accounting can only be carried out under a social system of production.

As long as industrial and technological decision-making power lies in the hands of the private owners, these decisions will continue to be made in the private interests of those owners, and the social costs of those decisions will never be taken into account. This can only change when industrial and economic decisions are made at the social level, not at the private level. The social control and transformation of technology cannot take place without social control over that technology, and thus social control over the economy, and this in turn demands a radical restructuring of the entire existing social and economic order. There must, in other words, be an environmental revolution.

The existing mainstream environmental organizations are unlikely to produce such a far-reaching and radical plan of action. Since its inception in the 1960's, the ecology movement has, for the most part, attracted white, financially-stable upper middle class, "leisure-oriented" people. As soon as they were formed, these ecology groups promptly found themselves under attack by the

New Left. The student group SDS boycotted "Earth Day" in 1970, saying that ecology was a "frivolous distraction" away from the Movement. Many Black Power groups called the environmental movement counter-productive, saying that it drew attention away from the struggle for liberation. When environmental students at San Jose State College buried a $2500 car to protest pollution, African-American groups picketed the ceremony, arguing that the money could have been better spent in helping the inner city poor.

"Not surprisingly," concludes ecological activist Murray Bookchin, "the New Left, like the Old Left, has never grasped the revolutionary potential of the ecology issue":

> At best, the issue is given lip service, with some drivel about how "pollution is profitable"; at worst, it is denounced as spurious, diversionary and "objectively counter-revolutionary".

The conservatism of the current generation of mainstream environmental organizations is apparent. Many middle-class ecologists see pollution as being caused by individual overconsumption, and urge others to consume less and "live simply". They do not explain how poor people can live any more simply than they already are.

Others have turned to the "Pogo" theory — "We have met the enemy, and he is us." These environmentalists urge us to ride bikes instead of cars, to use paper instead of styrofoam, and to replace dangerous chemicals in the home with safer products. Although this strategy may help to salve the conscience of middle-class consumers, it does virtually nothing to halt environmental degradation.

Even the corporations that produce most of the environmental damage have realized that ecology has become a useful selling tool. "Green" products, consisting of everything from "biodegradable" garbage bags to "tree-free" toilet paper and "environmentally-sound" disposable diapers, make up a rapidly-growing portion of corporate sales. Exxon, which dumped millions of gallons of crude off the shore of Alaska and then welshed on the cleanup, and DuPont, the largest producer of chemical poisons in the world, now advertise themselves as "environmentally-concerned". Executives and officers from many such corporations now sit on the boards of many of the mainstream conservation groups.

These environmental groups, meanwhile, busy themselves with mild legal campaigns to put meaningless (and often ignored) limits on pollution, while doing nothing about the corporate source of pollution. Groups like the World Wildlife Fund, the Sierra Club and the Audubon Society do nothing more than lobby for reform in Washington DC. William Reilly, a former President of the World Wildlife Fund, was appointed to head the Environmental Protection Agency under George HW Bush, who declared himself to be "The Environmental President". Meanwhile, the corporate polluters continued unabated.

Other environmental groups like Greenpeace and the Green Party, have not lost their militant goals, but have enmeshed themselves so deeply in existing political structures that they have little chance of achieving their aims. Already, the Green Parties in Europe have moved steadily towards "respectability" in order to maintain their electoral position (a tendency in turn being opposed — rather unsuccessfully — by the Left Green faction).

If the industrial and economic structures which produce environmental degradation are to be changed, they must be taken out of the hands of the private interests and placed under social control. This, of course, is where the programs of the Marxists and the environmentalists overlap. Marxism, however, has not had much to say about environmental issues.

Some radical environmentalists have noticed that Marx, even in his chosen emphasis on economic structures, failed to see the impact of environmental factors on the development of capitalist economics. The Marxian "means of production", they point out, are heavily dependent upon environmental energy sources. As the sources of energy changed during the 19th century (from wood to coal, and then from coal to oil), the machinery and technology of the means of production changed drastically. As Robert Paehkle puts it:

> Marx's "superstructure" may or may not rest on the forces and relations of production, on machines and organization. But clearly all these things do rest on something fleeting, on a fragile and temporary gift from the dead plant and animal species of aeons past.

The choice of economic machinery and technology, which plays a vital role in Marx's description of capitalism, is, Paehkle reminds us, in itself the product of a decision that involves ecological factors.

The basic Marxian attitude towards ecologists, Paehkle points out, is simple: "The socialist revolution will eliminate capitalism, capitalists are responsible for environmental damage, case closed." In the meantime, the Marxists declare, socialists should support the expansion of industry and economic growth, since a socialist economy can only be built in "advanced material conditions" — i.e., in a highly industrialized economy.

The Leninists likewise embrace the doctrine of rapid industrial development. The Revolutionary Communist Party speaks of taking over the capitalist forces of production, but is silent about how it intends to alter them to reduce their environmental impact:

> The highly developed productive forces and technological level in this country will be a real advantage for the proletariat; much of the physical capacity will remain, despite extensive destruction, and beyond that the knowledge and experience in creating and utilizing this technology will not be destroyed.

For the most part, Marxists and Leninists have paid little attention to the matter of de-industrialization, of altering industrial techniques in accordance with environmental concerns. As Paehkle says, "Under 'real' socialism, it is assumed, highways would not be built through prime farmland, automobiles would not pollute, and nuclear power plants would function safely."

The experiences of the Leninist nations have not been very reassuring on this point. Quite apart from the highly publicized accidents at Chernobyl and the near-destruction of Lake Baikal, the Leninist nations have been environmental disasters. The Soviet Union, East Germany, Poland and Czechoslovakia produced some of the most heavily polluted places on earth. Between 1922 and 1962, the amount of industrial wastes dumped into Soviet rivers increased nearly 2,000%. In the 1960's, *Pravda* described the pollution in the Dneiper River: "Many scenic places along the river banks are no longer suitable for purposes of relaxation and are a menace to health. The fish are disappearing." One of the sparks that set off the anti-Soviet rebellions in 1989 were Soviet plans to install new nuclear reactors and rad-waste dumps in the Baltic states.

"In general," Barry Commoner notes, "the modern technologies of the Soviet Union appear to be as counter-ecological as those introduced into the United States economy." Environmental destruction, then, does not appear to be unique to either capitalism or socialism.

Leninist groups in the United States have nevertheless, in the past few years, attempted to be "green" as well as "red". All of them, in an attempt to jump on the latest bandwagon, have added a concern for the environment to their laundry list of demands. In the environmental area that should appeal to them the most — within the workplace — the Leninists have been notably absent.

Traditional worker organizations, such as the trade unions, have, for the most part, paid more attention to wages and benefits than to environmental workplace safety issues. Many unionists have even opposed environmental restrictions on polluting industries, saying that such measures "cost jobs". As a result, workers in the US are being poisoned at an alarming rate.

Workers and poor people bear the brunt of environmental contamination, in the form of workplace exposure, air pollution, uncontrolled hazardous waste dumps, and illegal toxic waste disposal. No one is more directly or intensely exposed to dangerous chemicals than the workers who handle them. Often, such exposure continues long after the danger becomes apparent. The toxic chemicals composed of polychlorinated biphenyls (PCBs), for example, were first synthesized in the 1930's. Within the space of three years, it was noticed that workers who had been exposed to PCBs were developing health problems, but nothing was done to halt the contamination until the 1960's, after the chemical had already been widely released into the environment.

Workers who handled nuclear materials (especially for the military) were routinely exposed to radiation for years before anybody admitted that there was any danger. Coke-oven workers in steel mills inhale coal tar, and die at a rate ten times higher than their co-workers. Building and construction workers continued to install asbestos for years after the companies had already determined that the substance was dangerous.

Perhaps the most callous statement about workplace hazards was made by the National Peach Council in the 1970's, after the Carter Administration tried to restrict the use of the toxic pesticide DBCP (which causes sterility in those who are exposed). The peach industry, a heavy user of the chemical, responded:

> While involuntary sterility caused by a manufactured chemical may be bad, it is not necessarily so. After all, there are many people now paying to have themselves sterilized to assure that they will no longer be able to become parents. . . If possible sterility is the problem, couldn't workers who were old enough that they no longer wanted to have children accept such positions voluntarily? Or could workers be advised of the situation, and some might volunteer for such work posts as an alternative to planned surgery for a vasectomy or tubal ligation, or as a means of getting around religious bans on birth control?

To fight against proposed environmental restrictions, many corporations have presented their workers with a "jobs or the environment" dilemma, claiming that the cost of complying with environmental standards would bankrupt the company and put its workers out on the streets. During the Reagan years, the US

Government itself jumped in on this strategy. After the federal government imposed a cleanup order on an Asarco, Inc., copper smelter in Tacoma, Washington, the company declared it couldn't afford the cleanup and threatened to close its doors. EPA Director William Ruckelshaus obligingly allowed the city to make the choice between the jobs or the environmental protection. The city chose the jobs, only to have the plant go bankrupt and close down anyway in 1985.

The issue of the workplace environment even brought about some changes in the most hard-nosed of the neo-Malthusians, Earth First!. In 1987, a worker at a Louisiana-Pacific lumber mill was seriously injured when the band saw he was operating struck a tree spike and shattered. Although it seemed clear that the spike hadn't been the work of Earth First!, the incident touched off a debate about the group's avowed policy of "bio-centrism", which held that the life of a human being was no more important than that of any other organism. Bio-centrism, pointed out ecologist Harold Gilliam, easily produced the feeling that, "Although spiking could kill workers, it would serve them right for killing trees." The timber workers were, after all, the enemy.

An opposing faction within Earth First! was led by Judi Bari, a labor organizer who belonged to the "Wobblies", the Industrial Workers of the World. Bari began organizing the timber workers around workplace safety issues, and built bridges between the workers and the environmentalists by pointing out that, if all of the trees disappeared, so too did the workers' jobs. Bari immediately renounced any further use of tree spiking by Earth First!.

Bari's action was promptly denounced by the rest of the organization. EF!er Michael Robinson announced, "Equating the rights of victimized sawmill workers with the needs of ecosystems disempowers us from speaking clearly in the future about the ecosystem. . . Let someone else make these connections and alliances; it's not our job."

The split became final when EF! co-founder David Foreman left the group, charging that it had become taken over by "class-struggle leftists". Bari, for her part, countered, "Besides being a sell-out and a right-winger, Foreman doesn't know the meaning of the word 'solidarity'."

Bari made strides in forging a worker-environmentalist alliance to fight the timber companies. In Pennsylvania, another IWW branch worked to make connections between a local environmental organization and a group of cement workers who opposed the company's decision to use toxic hazardous waste as fuel for the cement kiln.

Recently, the radical environmental movement has been expanding its scope with a new message — that of interconnection and mutual interaction. Decades ago, the naturalist John Muir wrote, "When we try to pick out anything by itself, we find it hitched to everything else in the universe."

Muir was speaking of biological organisms, but modern activists have found that this principle applies to social conditions as well. Because of its tendency to illustrate the interconnectedness of social structures with environmental effects, ecology has sometimes been referred to as "the subversive science". "By pointing out the endless connections between everything," says activist Rik Scarce, "ecology subverts the dominant paradigm."

One of the most successful attempts to expand the relevance of environmental activism has been the French "eco-feminist" movement, which ties an analysis of industrial development with a condemnation of the patriarchical social structures which have encouraged environmental destruction. The IWW — environmentalist alliance, on the other hand, illustrates another kind of synthesis — a combination of ecological analysis with a criticism of the economic and social relationships of industrial capitalism. Through such interpenetrating outlooks, the environmental movement will be able to extend its reach to include nearly every sphere of modern society. "I think we need to realize," says Judi Bari, "how revolutionary what we're saying really is."

Marxian socialists, then, have much to discuss with the radical environmental movement. The changes in industry and technology which the environmentalists demand cannot be brought about without the assumption of social control over the production process. In this sense, no environmental revolution can take place without a socialist one.

On the other hand, Marxian socialism needs to recognize the crucial role which environmental relationships play in the construction of economic structures. As Robert Paehkle says, "A socialist – environmentalist synthesis would require a revision of socialism as fundamental as the revisions sustained by liberalism in the late 19th and early 20th century in the face of the socialist challenge." Socialism demands a corresponding environmental revolution for its success.

The introduction of environmentally-sound technologies demands drastic changes in the way that Marxists have traditionally viewed the process of economic decision-making. In essence, these ecological considerations must produce, not a centralized state planning structure which controls all economic resources, but instead a decentralized technological structure, with decision-making removed from central power and placed in local hands. This lesson of decentralized authority and ownership structures has much in common with the syndicalist and "council communist" schools of decentralized social control over the economy.

The Leninist program of state control, rapid industrialization and continuous economic expansion, it is clear, cannot be a part of a successful socialist program. In the aftermath of a successful environmental/socialist revolution, Marxists will still be faced with the tasks of replacing current environmentally-damaging technology with decentralized low-impact industrial systems. This can only be done through an alliance of socialist and environmental concerns.

We can see, then, that the radical environmental movement presents a threat to the bourgeois social order which is, in many ways, as great as the threat presented by the organized working class. In many ways, the radical environmental movement complements and supplements the radical socialist movement. Both call for economic and social decision-making to be taken out of the hands of the capitalist elite and returned to decentralized social control, so that people can make the decisions that affect their lives, directly and democratically.

These goals, in turn, overlap with yet another social movement that calls for the decentralization of decision-making power.

Anarchism

The longest-running (and, perhaps, the most bitter) debate within the social justice movement has been that between the Marxists and the anarchists. In the early history of the radical labor movement, anarchism and its variants were the single greatest competitor to Marxian socialism and, in Spain, Italy and France, anarchism and anarcho-syndicalism rose to domination over the Marxist "workers' parties".

The conflict between the Marxists and the anarchists centers around the role of authority and centralized control, particularly as it applies to the institution of the state. In the traditional Marxian view, the capitalist republic is a mere tool of the ruling class, and is used by the capitalists to safeguard their position of economic and social privilege. Marx writes that the modern state is "nothing more than the form of organization which the bourgeoisie necessarily adopt for the mutual guarantee of their property and interests."

Since the political state is the tool of the ruling class, Marx concluded, the way to overthrow the capitalists was to organize the working class and take over the state machinery, denying its use to the bourgeoisie and converting the state into an instrument of worker control over the economy. "We want the abolition of classes," Engels writes. "How can this be achieved? By the political domination of the proletariat." Marx echoes, "The conquest of political power is the first task of the proletariat." In an address to the Communist League in 1850, Marx declared that the revolutionary movement must strive towards "the most decisive centralization of power in the hands of the state authority."

Marx, as a revolutionary, firmly believed that, in most cases, the working class would never be able to capture the state except through violent rebellion. However, he always held out the possibility that the state could be captured through electoral politics in some countries, and was a tireless fighter for universal suffrage, concluding that the working class might be able to win at the ballot box if it could not win in the streets. "We do not deny," he told a gathering of Dutch radicals, "that there are countries such as America, England, and I would add Holland if I knew your institutions better, where the working people may achieve their goal by peaceful means." In any case, Marx concluded, the goal of the proletariat was, using whatever method was practical, to capture the machinery of government and turn it against the capitalists, placing it in the hands of a working-class dominated state.

Once the capitalist state was captured, the working class would be able to use this position of power to dismantle the old capitalist economic structures and install a new communist system in its place. Marx referred to this period of transition as "the dictatorship of the proletariat":

> Between capitalist and communist society lies a period of revolutionary transformation from one form to the other. There is a corresponding period of transition in the political sphere, and in this period the state can only take the form of a revolutionary dictatorship of the proletariat.

To the anarchists, this was complete heresy. In contrast to Marx, who argued that the domination of the state by the capitalists was a direct result of their economic domination of the working class, Mikhail Bakunin, a Russian radical, countered that it was the political domination of the bourgeoisie, through its state apparatus, that enabled it to exert economic control. Instead of wresting control of the state from the bourgeoisie and using it to dismantle capitalist economics, as Marx proposed, Bakunin advocated dismantling the entire state apparatus, and thus remove the bourgeoisie's ability to use coercion and authority to dominate economic relationships. "We believe," Bakunin countered, "that the policy of the proletariat, necessarily revolutionary, should have the destruction of the state for its immediate and only goal."

Bakunin bitterly attacked the Marxian program of state control of the economy (under the domination of the working class), arguing that such an authority structure would, even if formed with the best of intentions, inevitably lead to a new form of economic domination. In a prescient passage, Bakunin predicted:

> The leaders of the Communist Party, namely Mr. Marx and his followers, will proceed to liberate humanity in their own way. They will concentrate the reins of government in a strong hand . . . under the direct command of state engineers, who will constitute a new privileged scientific and political class.

To Bakunin, the existence of any state, even a "proletarian" one, was intolerable: "The trouble lies not in any particular form of government, but in the very existence of government itself."

The conflict between the Marxists and the Bakuninists began to boil over in 1864, when Bakunin, while visiting Marx in Paris, was invited to join Marx's International Workingmen's Association (the First International). Bakunin viewed the International as a small, poorly organized group, and instead formed his own organization, the Alliance of Revolutionary Socialists. While the International continued to advocate worker control of government as the first step towards communism, Bakunin's Alliance followed an anarchist program of opposition to all state power.

In 1867, Bakunin became a member of the Central Committee of the Pacifist League for Peace and Freedom, and tried to take over the group by packing it with Alliance supporters. The attempt failed just as the militant strikes of 1867-1868 broke out. Bakunin turned to the International.

The first tiff to occur between Marx and Bakunin concerned the affiliation of the Alliance of Revolutionary Socialists with the International. Bakunin wanted the entire Alliance to be admitted as a bloc, but Marx and the International, fearing another takeover attempt, instead demanded that the Alliance dissolve itself and join the International's various national sections. Reluctantly, Bakunin agreed to this.

Instead of disbanding, however, the Alliance continued to function as a caucus, and began to take steps to dominate the International and change it over to a Bakuninist program. First, Bakunin attempted to pack the International's Central Council with his supporters. When he discovered that he would not be able to obtain a majority on the Council, he then argued for its disbandment, and concentrated his efforts on winning over the various national sections. In 1872, Bakunin was formally expelled from the International on the grounds that he had not disbanded the Alliance of Revolutionary Socialists as he had agreed.

Much of the debate between Marx and Bakunin centered around such pedantic nonsense as the definition of "authority", or whether political actions by the workers should be avoided because it legitimizes the state. Much of the argument degenerated into petty name-calling and bureaucratic intrigue — Bakunin referred to Marx as "vain, perfidious and cunning", described Engels as "adept at calumny, lying and intrigue", and accused both of them of "boasting in theory and cowardice in practice". Marx, for his part, referred to Bakunin as a "nonentity as a theoretician", ridiculed his "papal authority", and labeled his anarchist outlooks "petty bourgeois". On several occasions, Marx repeated some old rumors that Bakunin was a Tsarist agent who had been sent to disrupt the radical movement.

Amidst all the invective, however, some important points managed to be raised and discussed. Bakunin pointed out that, in nearly every country, the industrial working class was far outnumbered by the peasantry and the agrarian workers. He vehemently rejected Marx's claim that the industrial working class had to be the agents of communist revolution, and instead argued that revolution could come only from the countryside.

Marx, in turn, pointed out that Bakunin had not resolved the question of precisely how any organization, much less the loose, anti-authoritarian one proposed by the anarchists, could ever bring about a revolution. As a part of his revolutionary program, Bakunin had written:

> The constructive tasks of the social revolution, the new forms of social life, can emerge only from the living experience of the grass-roots organizations which will themselves build the new society according to their manifold needs and desires.

Noble sentiments, Marx admitted, but, he asked, how was a loose organization going to defeat the highly centralized and militarized capitalist state?

Bakunin himself grappled repeatedly with this question, and never fully answered it. The only solution he ever reached was, in light of his professed libertarianism, surprising:

> For revolution to triumph over reaction, the unity of revolutionary thought and action must have an organ in the midst of the popular anarchy which will be the way of life and source of all the energy of the revolution. . . Our aim is the creation of a powerful but always invisible revolutionary association which will prepare and direct the revolution.
>
> Ten, twenty, or thirty men, with a clear understanding and good organization, knowing what they want and where they are going, can easily carry with them a hundred, two hundred, three hundred or even more.

Bakunin's proposal for a small revolutionary elite that would direct the revolution sounds suspiciously like Lenin's argument for the "vanguard party" which would carry out the revolution in behalf of the workers. Despite all of his libertarian and anti-authoritarian talk, in the end Bakunin was unable to move beyond the notion that the revolutionary elite would make the revolution, with the masses or without them.

In essence, then, the Bakunin/Marx argument centered around a fundamental question which the revolutionary movement has still not settled — does a revolutionary organization derive its power from a broad decentralized base or from a pyramidical centralized structure?

The question was first put to a practical test in 1870, when the city of Paris rose in revolt and established the Paris Commune. Both Marx and Bakunin studied the Commune intently, and both were heavily influenced by it.

In 1871, the working class of Paris succeeded in creating a revolutionary government that held power for a short time before being brutally and bloodily suppressed. And the very first act it carried out, much to Marx's surprise, was to abandon the old governmental apparatus and build an entirely new political system. Marx writes:

> From the outset, the Commune was compelled to recognize that the working class, once come to power, could not manage with the old state machine; that in order not to lose again its only just-conquered supremacy, the working class must, on the one hand, do away with all the old repressive machinery, previously used against itself, and on the other hand, safeguard itself against its own deputies and officials by declaring them all, without exception, subject to recall at any moment.

Engels viewed the Commune as a "shattering of the former state power and its replacement by a new and really democratic state", and concluded that it was "no longer a state in the proper sense of the word." Bakunin, elated, viewed the Commune as a confirmation of his anti-state outlooks, and declared the Commune to be "a bold, clearly-formulated negation of the state".

Not all governmental functions, however, disappeared under the Commune. There was still a need for such things as record-keeping and the enforcement of common criminal laws. These functions were, however, stripped of their political and class functions. Marx writes admiringly:

> While the merely repressive organs of the old governmental power were to be amputated, its legitimate functions were to be wrested from an authority usurping pre-eminence over society itself, and restored to the responsible agents of society.
>
> Against the transformation of the state and the agents of the state from the servants of society into the masters of society — an inevitable transformation in all previous states — the Commune made use of two infallible expedients. In the first place, it filled all posts — administrative, judicial and educational — by election on the basis of universal suffrage of all concerned, with the right of these same electors to recall their delegates at any time. And in the second place, all officials, high or low, were paid only the wages received by other workers.

The Commune was an important event for Marx and Engels. Until 1871, they had assumed that the working class would be able to seize the existing institutions of the bourgeois republic and use them as the basis for a socialist government after the revolution.

The Commune, however, completely changed Marx's thinking on this point, and made such a profound impact on him that he added an amendment to the *Communist Manifesto* on the matter. Marx also wrote an entire manuscript on the Commune, entitled *The Civil War in France*. The Commune was, he concluded, "the political form at last discovered under which to work out the economic emancipation of labor."

Apparently, the Commune didn't influence Engels as much as it did Marx. After Marx's death, Engels went back to his criticisms of anarchism and instead advocated capturing the state through the election of a social democratic party.

The anarchist movement, meanwhile, began to turn away from organization and towards individual actions which defied the authority of the state, including the assassination of political figures. The motto of this movement of "propaganda of the deed" was put most succinctly by the Russian anarchist Peter Kropotkin: "Anything suits us that is alien to legality". For the most part, these individual actions accomplished nothing more than killing a few government officials and landing many anarchists in jail.

Within a few years, Kropotkin realized that the anarchist assassins were merely isolating themselves from the working class and accomplishing nothing. It was an "illusion", he concluded, to believe that "one can defeat the coalition of exploiters with a few pounds of explosives". Instead, Kropotkin now argued, "One must be with the people, who no longer want isolated acts, but want men of action inside their ranks." The individualist "propaganda of the deed" began to fade away, to be replaced by the collective anarchists or "anarcho-communists". In Europe, the most militant of the collective anarchists were the council communists.

The framework of the worker's council was born in the turbulent upheavals in Europe between 1917 and 1920. In the wake of the Russian Revolution in 1917, a wave of radicalism swept over Europe. In February 1919, the Italian Federation of Metal Workers (FIOM) won a contractual right to form "Internal Commissions" of worker delegates in the factories. The militant metal workers then used a series of strikes and shutdowns to turn the Commissions into de facto managers, with the workers themselves running the plant through their elected representatives. Within a period of two years, the industrial workers of Turin and Genoa had seized a number of factories and paralyzed the authorities with a general strike.

In Germany, at the same time, the German Communist Party (KPD) split away from the German Communist Workers Party (KAPD) and began advocating *Rate Kommunismus*, or "council communism". The KPD allied itself with a similar group in Holland, centered around the Dutch astronomer Anton Pannekoek. Pannekoek praised the worker's councils, saying:

> The goal of the working class is liberation from exploitation. This goal is not reached and cannot be reached by a new directing and

governing class substituting itself for the bourgeoisie. It is only realized by the workers themselves being master over production.

In Germany, the government tottered on the brink of collapse, as strikes and worker uprisings came within a hair's breadth of seizing power. In Hungary, the government actually fell, and a "Soviet Government" held power for a short time. In all of these militant movements, the instrument of organization was the worker's council, an elected body of workers from each plant who organized and carried out the rebellions. In many ways, the worker's councils echoed the organizational structures of the Paris Commune.

The council communists realized that the power of the bourgeoisie could not be broken as long as they controlled the state apparatus. However, they also realized that the workers would have to develop their own organizational methods to carry out the process of economic production and re-distribution. The Social Democrats, echoing Marx and Engels, still advocated capturing the existing state through electoral campaigns and then legislating for government ownership of industries — their definition of "socialism".

This strategy was attacked by the council communists. "'Statifying' companies," Pannekoek declared, "is not socialism; socialism is the power of the proletariat." The Italian council communist Antonio Gramsci wrote that the worker's councils were "organs suited to future communist management of both the individual factory and the whole society".

Similar ideas were being tried in Russia. In 1917, the Russians had deposed the Tsar and the Provisional Government by organizing into *soviets* (from the Russian word for "council"). Throughout the new Soviet Union, anarchist and syndicalist workers were deposing their bosses and running the industries themselves, through elected worker Soviets. In Georgia, the anarchist Nestor Makhno set up a government of elected councils over a huge area.

The European council communists at first praised Lenin's Bolsheviks and their Soviet form of government, believing it to be based on the direct democratic control of the workplace by worker's councils. The Dutch communist Hermann Gorter pronounced, "This supple and flexible organism is the world's first socialist regime." The Italian anarchist Camillo Berneri declared the Soviets to be "the most practical experiment in integral democracy on the largest scale yet attempted."

Lenin's centralized Bolsheviks, however, did not tolerate the libertarian syndicalists for very long. Within a few years, it had become apparent that the Bolsheviks would carry the old Marxian dictum of "dictatorship of the proletariat" to its extreme. Rather than allowing the factories to continue to be run by elected worker's councils, Lenin deposed the Soviets and centralized all political and economic control in the hands of his central state. Lenin turned the entire state apparatus to the single-minded goal of expanding industrial output, and regimented the working class for this task far more ruthlessly than the capitalists ever could have. Lenin declared:

> A condition for economic revival is the raising of the working people's discipline, their skills, their effectiveness, the intensity of labor and its better organization. . . We must raise the question of piecework and apply and test it in practice; we must raise the question of applying much of what is scientific and progressive in the Taylor system.

In an incredibly frank assessment, Lenin declared that communism consisted of "nothing but state capitalist monopoly made to benefit the whole people. . . For a certain time, the workers' state cannot be other than a bourgeois state without the bourgeoisie." To the anarchists and the council communists, Lenin's intentions were brutally clear; workplace democracy would have to wait. In the meantime, get back to work.

Word began to filter back to Europe about the Bolshevik brand of "democratic centralism". In 1920, when Otto Rühle toured the Soviet Union as a delegate to the Second Congress of the Communist International, he reported that the Soviets were mere tools of the ruling Bolshevik Party, and were "not councils in a revolutionary sense". Instead, he pointed out, the Leninists were ruling through "bureaucracy, the deadly enemy of the council system."

The Italian anarchist Malatesta condemned the Bolsheviks as a "new government which has set itself up above the Revolution in order to bridle it and subject it to the purposes of a particular party." Pannekoek wrote:

> If the most important element of the revolution consists in the masses taking their own affairs — the management of society and production — in hand themselves, then any form of organization which does not permit control and direction by the masses themselves is counter-revolutionary and harmful.

When the Bolsheviks, through the Third International, began to mold the other Communist Parties to their own image, the council movement responded with calls for internal democracy and rank-and-file control of the Party. Antonio Gramsci, from his prison cell in Italy, criticized the Italian Communists, calling for "a greater intervention of the proletarian elements in the life of the party and a diminution of the powers of the bureaucracy."

Hermann Gorter bluntly declared, "The Russian tactics of dictatorship by party and leadership cannot possibly be correct here." Berneri labeled the Leninists as "a new state, inevitably centralized and authoritarian". Lenin responded to all of these criticisms with a work entitled *Left-Wing Communism; An Infantile Disorder*, which attacked Pannekoek and the council communists as "anarchist" and "undisciplined".

In 1921, when the sailors at the Kronstadt Fortress mutinied and workers in Petrograd struck in an attempt to overthrow the Bolsheviks and re-institute the Soviets and direct worker control, the council communists cheered them on. Alexander Berkman declared, "Kronstadt blew sky high the myth of the proletarian state; it proved that the dictatorship of the Communist Party and the Revolution were really incompatible." "Now that the proletariat has risen up against you, the communist party," Gorter wrote, "now that you have had to declare a state of emergency in Petrograd against the proletariat . . . has the thought still not occurred to you, even now, that dictatorship by the proletariat is really preferable to dictatorship by the party?" Gorter bitterly concluded:

> Your real fault, which neither we nor history can forgive, is to have foisted a counter-revolutionary program and tactics upon the world proletariat, and to have rejected the really revolutionary ones which could have saved us.

The protests of the council movement were in vain, however. The Bolsheviks succeeded in imposing a program of "21 Points" upon the Communist International parties, which effectively reduced them to instruments of Stalin's Central Committee. The "left-wing" council communists were expelled from the party, and most went into exile and obscurity. The ruling Bolsheviks removed the last vestiges of the Soviet government, crushed rank-and-file rebellions led by the Kronstadt sailors and by the Ukrainian councilist Makhno, and expelled and purged the councilist "Worker's Opposition" within the Communist Government. By 1925, the council communist movement had all but ceased to exist.

Today, the Marxist-Leninist parties still advocate a system of rigid economic control by a centralized government. The Revolutionary Communist Party, while rejecting electoral politics, nevertheless declares that the seizure of the political state is the first step towards revolution:

> There can be no such thing as socialism in one factory, or in one part of society. . . The socialist revolution has to be a conscious act whereby the proletariat takes control of the superstructure through a political revolution, and only then can begin to establish the new socialist productive relations.

> The basic first step of the proletariat, having won political power, is to take into its hands, through its state and the leadership of the its party, the decisive levers and lifelines of the economy. . . In short, it socializes ownership of the major means of production and institutes basic overall planning of the economy in accordance with this, through the proletarian state.

Modern anarchists and syndicalists have applied the same criticisms to the Leninist reliance on state control as Bakunin had applied to Marx. The Spanish anarchist Angel Pestana bluntly concludes, "The revolution is not, and cannot be, the work of a party. The most a party can do is foment a coup d'etat. But a coup d'etat is not a revolution." Eco-anarchist Murray Bookchin echoes:

> The party is structured along hierarchical lines that reflect the very society it professes to oppose. Despite its theoretical pretensions, it is a bourgeois organism, a miniature state, with an apparatus and a cadre whose function is to seize power, not dissolve power.

Anarchists point with alarm at the hierarchical structure of the Leninist parties, and at the rampant thought control and repression that permeates Leninist states. Bakunin, we might conclude, may have exaggerated the authoritarian aspect of Marx's strategy, but his fears came completely to life in Leninism.

It is not correct to say, however, that the authoritarian and repressive aspects of Leninism resulted solely from its Marxian theoretical base. There are pressing economic reasons why the Leninist state was inexorably drawn into rigid centralized control. In every instance, Leninist parties came to power in nations with underdeveloped economies, and the first task of the Leninist state had to be to develop an industrial base as rapidly as possible. This could only have been done by a central state authority that monopolized all economic resources, and that rigorously planned their development to produce the swiftest growth possible. In a very real sense, it was the lack of economic resources, rather than any political or ideological causes, that compelled the Leninists to resort to central state authority.

The conflict between the Marxists and the Bakuninists can be seen, then, at its most basic level, to center around the problem of economic scarcity. The assumed "scarcity of resources" lies at the very heart of capitalism. If there are not enough economic resources to go around, some method must be found to decide who gets access to them and who must go without. Under capitalism, ownership of property decides this—wealthy people have unlimited access to resources, while poor people have severely limited access.

To be successful, socialism must have at its disposal sufficient economic resources to insure that every member of society can be provided for, and this can only take place in an economy where productivity and economic ability are extremely high. Marx, however, was writing at a time when the productive forces of capitalism were just beginning to develop, and no one could be sure how quickly or how far this productive capacity would be able to expand. Marx was able to see the potentially rapid expansion of resources under capitalism, but he never saw the actual immense productive ability which developed under monopoly corporatism.

Marx, based on the studies he made at the time, expected that capitalism would never be able to fully develop its productive abilities on its own. This was not because he doubted capitalism's capacity to continually expand its economic resources, but because he believed he was witnessing the contradictions and stresses that would soon tear capitalism apart. Until the end of his life, Marx expected that the socialist revolution would come very soon, and thus remove capitalism before it had a chance to fully develop its productive forces on its own.

Since, he assumed, capitalism would die before it was able to produce an economy of super-abundance, Marx expected that it would fall upon the socialist revolution to accomplish this task. After the revolution, Marx thought, the working class would have to carry out this task of expanding productive ability on its own. It would also have to carry out the process of fully integrating political and economic functions into one administrative apparatus, and developing these various structures into the communist mode of production.

This process of economic development, if it was to be done under the guidance of the working class, had to be accomplished through economic planning, and this necessitated a central authority which controlled and allocated all economic resources. This socialist system, Marx concluded, would have to remain until the planning apparatus was able to accomplish its task and produce the highly developed productive forces which were necessary for a communist system. Marx thus argued in favor of a period of "socialism" — a government of the proletariat — which would carry out the process of economic expansion before dying off and allowing "communism" to take over.

After the Paris Commune, Marx decided that the old bourgeois state apparatus was not suitable for the working class's purposes, and that the workers would have to introduce their own transitional governmental structure; one which would be able to take control of the nation's economic resources and expand them to the necessary levels.

Marx's conflict with Bakunin centered around the structure of this "dictatorship of the proletariat". In essence, Marx wanted to use a working class government to develop the productive forces which would be left by capitalism until they were strong enough for the super-abundance necessary for communist economic relationships. Bakunin, on the other hand, wanted to develop productive forces using independent communes, not a central planning apparatus administered by a socialist state.

The Leninists, who took power in a country that was economically weak and undeveloped, found the Marxian idea of the central "proletarian state" to be perfectly suited for their need for rapid industrialization. They were thus able to use Marxist phraseology to justify their centrally-planned industrialization program, which developed high productive levels in the economy, but did it in the class interests of the bureaucrats rather than the working class.

In retrospect, we can see that Marx was wrong, as modern capitalist development has made much of his reasoning irrelevant. Today, capitalism itself has already developed extraordinarily high levels of productivity, and has increased economic capacity far beyond anything which Marx could have imagined.

Given the incredible output that could result from the full utilization of our current productive capacity, it seems possible for an industrialized society to produce all of its needs while utilizing only a fraction of its present work force. Farming and food production has already undergone such an explosion of productivity under capitalism. While, under feudalism, nearly every member of society was engaged in producing food, under capitalism the impact of machinery has produced a society where more than enough food can be produced using only 5% of the population.

Similarly, manufacturing ability has expanded to the point where most people simply do not need to produce anything. The rise in employment in such non-manufacturing areas as service, advertising, sales and entertainment makes it clear that it is no longer necessary for a majority of the population to work in order to produce the economic necessities of life. In addition, the capitalist trend towards greater use of computer and robot technology introduces a means of reducing the working population still further, by replacing the human worker with machinery, automation and robot factories.

As Murray Bookchin puts it, "The Marxian critique is rooted in the past, in the era of material want and relatively limited technological development." The Leninists, by advocating a society of "full employment", demonstrate that they, too, are still caught in the illusions of scarcity. Instead of fighting for full employment, revolutionaries can begin to fight for a leisure society of full *un*-employment, without sacrificing any of our material standard of living.

There is, then, no need anymore to postulate a "socialist" state which replaces the capitalist state with a "dictatorship of the proletariat". It is not necessary to plan for a rapid expansion of productive ability after the revolution, because modern monopoly capitalism has already produced it, and has already brought about the development of an economy of super-abundance.

Today, the tasks of a socialist revolution consist of replacing bourgeois institutions and structures with social-ist ones, with new relationships of social hegemony that can carry on communist production and distribution from the start. The social relationships which carry out these tasks must be rooted in the institutions which were used by the working class to carry out the revolution; in other words, the revolutionary bodies must be capable of serving as the nucleus of the communist system.

In this manner, Marxism and anarcho-syndicalism can both be seen to be merely differing approaches to solving the same problem — that of building and running a social-ist society. As Bookchin concludes, "What we must create to replace bourgeois society is not only the classless society envisioned by socialism, but the nonrepressive utopia envisioned by anarchism."

The council communists believe that the political and social principles of anarchism and syndicalism must be combined with the socio-economic analysis of Marxism to become truly proletarian in character and to be capable of guiding the working class to liberation. Marxism provides the intellectual and theoretical weapons — a conception of how capitalism works and how social change develops. Syndicalism, on the other hands, provides the material weapons for the struggle — the general strike, militant direct action, industrial organization. Thus, syndico-Marxism, rather than Marxism-Leninism, is the only working class outlook which can produce the socialist mode of production.

The Leninist vanguard party is not well-suited to the self-liberation of the working class, and the revolutionary movement must reject it as a model. The most practical form of organization for the task of worker self-emancipation is that envisioned by Marx and practiced by the syndicalists — the organization of the worker's council.

Ideology

Marxism grew out of the tradition of philosophical materialism, which holds that thoughts and ideas are the products of material circumstances. It is not surprising, then, that in his writings Marx rarely mentions the effects of ideology and ideological struggles, except as part of his criticisms of philosophical idealism.

In contrast to the German ideologists, Marx declared that philosophical ideas and theories were mere abstractions, and could not be trusted to give an accurate picture of human society:

> Just as one does not judge an individual by what he thinks about himself, so one cannot judge such a period of transformation by its consciousness, but, on the contrary, this consciousness must be explained from the contradictions of material life.

Marx concluded that the thoughts which humans have about the world is a part of that world, and that ideology is a component of social reality just as economics, politics and family structures are:

> The production of ideas, of conceptions, of consciousness, is at first directly interwoven with the material activity and the material

intercourse of man, the language of real life. Conceiving, thinking, the mental intercourse of humans, appears at this stage as the direct efflux of their material behavior. The same applies to mental production as expressed in the language of politics, laws, morality, religion, metaphysics, etc., of a people. Humans are the producers of their conceptions, ideas, etc. — real, active humans, as they are conditioned by a definite development of their productive forces and of the intercourse corresponding to these, up to its furthest forms. Consciousness can never be anything else than conscious existence, and the existence of humans is their actual life-process.

Engels adds:

If the further question is raised; what then are thought and consciousness, and whence they come, it becomes apparent that they are products of the human brain and that humans themselves are products of Nature, which have been developed in and along with their environment.

Marx illustrates the interaction of ideology with material reality through the use of an analogy:

Upon the different forms of property, upon the social conditions of existence, rises an entire superstructure of distinct and peculiarly formed sentiments, illusions, modes of thought and views of life. The entire class creates and forms them out of its material foundations and out of the corresponding social relations.

"Thinking and being," Marx summarized, "are thus certainly distinct, but at the same time, they are in unity with each other":

The imaginary creations of the human brain are the inevitable sublimations of the material process of existence, which can be observed empirically and which depends on material causes. Morality, religion, metaphysics, and all other forms of ideology and the related forms of consciousness thus lose the independence they appear to have. They have no history or development of their own; it is only people, developing their material production and mutual material relations, who as a result come to think different thoughts and create different intellectual systems.

As writer Thomas Sowell points out, "Marx's theory of history was based on a principle later applied in physics by Einstein — that the position of the observer is an integral part of the data." And, since each class of people in human society is in a different social position, each will experience a different viewpoint and ideological outlook on what they observe.

Thus, Marx concluded, there are no "objective" ideas. Ideological or philosophical arguments over what actions are really "true" or "just" are irrelevant, since "truth" and "justice" are only what humans make of them — the definition of "justice" varies according to the changing social circumstances of the human beings who are attempting to define it. As Marx says:

> The whole problem of the transition from thought to reality, and thus from language to life, exists only as a philosophical illusion; it is justified only to the philosophic mind, puzzling over the origin and nature of its supposed detachment from real life.

Marx did realize, however, that ideological conflict was a fact of life in any class-divided society. Since the ruling class creates and maintains the social structure that allows it to thrive, existing socio-economic relationships reflect its interests. And, since ideas and theories tend to conform to existing social structures and frameworks, the majority of the intellectual outlooks which are developed in bourgeois society tend to accept bourgeois social conditions as a "given", and thus tend to reinforce and preserve them. As Marx writes:

> The ideas of the ruling class are in every epoch the ruling ideas, i.e., the class which is the ruling material force of society is at the same time its ruling intellectual force. . . The ruling ideas are nothing more than the ideal expression of the dominant material relationships, the dominant material relationships grasped as ideas; hence of the relationships which make the one class the ruling one, therefore, the ideas of its dominance.

The Marxian view of ideology, then, is consistent with the dialectical and naturalist philosophical view held by Marx;

existing social conditions are the framework within which ideas and theories must arise, but these ideas and theories are at the same time a component of these conditions, and can act to change them. In this manner, Marx writes, ideas themselves can become a force that alters existing social reality: "The weapon of criticism cannot, of course, replace criticism by weapons—material force must be overthrown by material force; but theory also becomes a material force as soon as it has gripped the masses." Thus, "theory" and "practice" are not separate things, but two poles of a single interrelationship.

After Marx's death, his dialectical viewpoint was abandoned and replaced by the "scientific Marxist" or "economic determinist" framework. In this point of view (and particularly in that variant of it that was codified by the Leninists), the distinction between "base" and "superstructure" mentioned by Marx was taken literally; the economic base directly determines the ideological superstructure, and ideology has no impact on human affairs—ideas and theories are simply automatic "reflections" of the thinker's economic conditions. As writer Carl Boggs puts it:

> In stressing the role of objective conditions, scientific Marxism accepted as axiomatic the notion that politics, ideology and culture were reflections of the material "base"—i.e., that they were elements of the "superstructure". Subjectivity was regarded as mere "appearance", with little independent or continuous existence of its own; ideology was thus understood as the distorted expression of social reality, as a form of rationalization or "false consciousness".

This concept of "false consciousness" plays a crucial role in the Leninist view of social change.

Leninist economic determinism held that human thoughts and ideas are derived from the specific economic circumstances within which these humans find themselves. This point of view takes literally Marx's aphorism, "It is not consciousness that determines life, but life that determines consciousness."

Since economic systems are divided into classes, and each of these classes finds itself in a different set of economic circumstances in relation to each other, these differing economic circumstances must, according to this view, produce in each class a distinct thought pattern and ideology consistent with their distinct economic conditions. In capitalist society, the owners are driven by their economic circumstances to defend capitalism, while the workers are driven by their differing economic circumstances to embrace socialism.

When the Leninists looked at the socialist movement as it existed shortly before World War I, however, they could find only the reformist Social Democratic Parties – the militant revolutionary movement was small, weak and cut off from the masses of working people. In the period 1917-1921, when social upheavals broke out in Italy, Germany and Hungary, revolutionary communist hopes that "the revolution" had at last begun were dashed by the death of these movements, brought about by a lack of mass involvement and broad popular support for militant organization.

In order to explain why the workers were so unwilling to embrace revolutionary communism despite the fact that, according to economic determinism, their economic positions should force them to do so, the Leninists had to resort to the concept of "false ideology". The working class's rejection of revolutionary communism, it was argued, is caused by a "false consciousness" which is imposed upon them by outsiders, and which these workers accept as their own. Rosa Luxemburg argued that the German, Italian and Hungarian revolutions had failed because the Social Democratic leaders had "betrayed" the workers, and had led them into the false ideology of liberal reformism. Lenin argued that the working class movement had been led astray by the trade union movement, which had produced an "aristocracy of labor" whose interests were closer to the capitalists than to the workers. All of the Third International Communists concluded that the capitalists had succeeded in corrupting the working class movement, infecting it with a "false consciousness" which hid from them their "real" interests.

This conclusion became the starting point for the Leninist theory of revolution. Lenin ruefully concluded that "false consciousness" and ideological corruption had forever removed the revolutionary potential of the working class. As he says:

> The history of all countries shows that the working class, exclusively by its own efforts, is able to develop only trade union consciousness, i.e., the conviction that it is necessary to combine in unions, fight the employers, and strive to compel the government to pass necessary labor legislation, etc.
>
> Since there can be no talk of an independent ideology formulated by the working masses themselves in the process of their movement, the only choice is—either bourgeois or socialist ideology.

This left the Leninists with a dilemma; if workers could not develop a revolutionary class consciousness on their own, how then were they ever to attain it and thus make the revolution? Lenin's answer was simple—the workers would obtain their revolutionary consciousness by having it brought to them by a dedicated core of communist theorists, by what he called "professional revolutionaries, irrespective of whether they have developed from among students or working men".

This is the basis for the "Marxist-Leninist Party", the elite cadre of trained dialectical materialists who interpret the economic laws which govern human society and who train the "backward sections of the masses" in these insights, all the while protecting them from "demagogues" who would lead them astray into the path of "false consciousness". The Leninist parties do not aim to interpret the working class's ideology—rather, they aim to create and control it. Thus the slogan of the Revolutionary Communist Party; "Create public opinion, seize power!"

The Leninist viewpoint was attacked vehemently by the section of the revolutionary movement that came to be known as "left-wing communists", "neo-Hegelian communists" or, more commonly, "council communists". Rather than a paternalistic party acting on behalf of the working class, the council communists called for worker self-emancipation, using the ideologies and direct actions developed by the rank and file workers.

Lenin, the council communists pointed out, assumed that human ideas had no impact at all on the development of human society; they were mere reflections of changes which had already taken place in the economic sphere, and were doomed to follow slavishly behind these economic changes. This was a return to the "mechanistic materialism" which had been criticized by Marx and Engels, who never believed that theories and ideologies had no impact on social development. It was a mistake, Engels declared, to assert that "because we deny an independent historical development to the various ideological spheres which play a part in history, we also deny them an effect upon history."

Ideas, Engels writes, could not be simple reflections of existing economic relationships. Any ideological system, he notes, "must not only correspond to the general economic position and be its expression, but must also be an expression which is consistent in itself, and which does not, owing to inner contradictions, look glaringly inconsistent. And in order to achieve this, the faithful reflection of economic conditions is more and more infringed upon."

Other critics have also attacked the Leninist reliance on "economic determinism" and "false consciousness", saying the two concepts are inconsistent with each other. The Leninists assert that the lack of proletarian class consciousness is brought about by the superimposition upon them of a "false ideology" by the capitalists. By asserting this, however, the Leninists are depicting the workers' ideology as coming from some place other than their own economic circumstances — they are seen as products of the capitalists' economic situation, not the workers'. The admission that the workers are capable of accepting an ideology that not only does not reflect their own economic class interests, but is actually in conflict with them, can only lead to the conclusion that the ideology of the working class is not determined by their economic circumstances, and necessitates the rejection of economic determinism.

Further, in order for workers to fall victim to a "false consciousness", there must exist some "true consciousness" which the workers "should" possess instead. The concept of a "true ideology", however, is subject to the very same criticisms which Marx heaped upon the philosophers and their notions of eternal Truth and Justice — the concept is a-historical and fails to take into account the effects of changing social conditions. As Steven Shulman puts it:

> The presumption is that workers have some identifiable set of objective interests, that these interests all coincide, that Marxists accurate recognize them, and that the workers unfortunately don't.
> These presumptions render the concept of false consciousness inherently idealist; objective interests, after all, are as variable as the possibilities for the future, and therefore can only be specified with respect to a hope or a belief about how the future will unfold.

Ironically, in their "economic determinist" attempts to discount the effects of ideology on human society, the Leninists have in effect created their own ideology and have decided what the working class "should" think. The Leninist high priests have thus effectively closed off any analysis of capitalist society that does not fit in with their orthodox framework. As the Italian council communist Antonio Gramsci points out, "The deterministic, fatalistic and mechanistic element has been a direct ideological 'aroma', emanating from the philosophy of praxis, rather like religion or drugs in its stupefying effects."

Rather than viewing the ideological struggle as a mere sub-category of the economic class struggle, the council communists have come to view both as an interpenetrating part of the other. All social relationships and ideologies, the council communists concluded, form a network of domination, which they referred to as a "hegemony". If this hegemony is to be overcome and overthrown, then all of its facets must be attacked and undermined — and, since ideologies form a part of this social web, they must be attacked and undermined as well. Gramsci notes:

For the philosophy of praxis, ideologies are anything but arbitrary; they are real historical facts which must be combatted and their nature as instruments of domination revealed, not for reasons of morality, etc., but for reasons of political struggle: in order to make the governed intellectually independent of the governing, in order to destroy one hegemony and create another.

Together with the problem of gaining political and economic power, the proletariat must also face the problem of winning intellectual power. Just as it has thought to organize itself politically and economically, it must also think about organizing itself culturally.

By rejecting the Leninist notions of "economic determinism" and "false ideology", the council communists were thereby forced to examine the capitalist "intellectual mode of production", the process whereby the ruling class controls and directs the process of conceptualization and theorizing in order to prevent an alternative conception from being established.

The process of intellectual hegemony falls, naturally enough, to the "intellectuals", those who deal with abstract concepts, theories and ideas. In capitalist society, the category "intellectuals" includes such diverse occupations as psychologists, writers, motion picture producers, artists, educators and teachers, scientists, philosophers, political theorists and anyone else who has the fundamental task of transferring ideas or outlooks from one person to another. "These intellectuals are the dominant group's 'deputies'," says Gramsci, "exercising the subaltern functions of social hegemony and political government." It is the intellectuals and the philosophers who have the role of justifying the world-view of the ruling class and of moderating that of the oppressed classes.

It is important to note that "hegemony" does not mean mere propaganda. Many times, the intellectuals who help to justify bourgeois social relationships are not even consciously aware that they are doing so — they may believe that their line of thought is completely independent of existing social structures, yet by accepting certain portions of the existing intellectual paradigm as "given", the effect of their intellectual activity is to support the existing social order.

Nuclear physicists, for example, are not overtly political in their goals, but by accepting the intellectual frameworks of "natural laws" and "cause and effect", they implicitly give weight to the capitalist view of economics as determined by the "invisible hand" of the "impersonal laws of the marketplace". Biologists, by accepting the Darwinian notion that biological development is brought about through impersonal processes of evolution, accept and support the bourgeois notion that humans have little control over the direction of their social development within the natural process.

Psychologists and psychiatrists sincerely believe that they are attempting to cure the mentally ill by helping them to "adjust" to society. By accepting the present form of "society" as a given and by "treating" any "maladjusted" persons who reject it, however, psychiatry gives support to the bourgeois ideology that capitalism is the best of all possible worlds and that it is those individuals who reject it which must be cured, not the social conditions which bring about this dissatisfaction.

The institutions of education are, of course, vital in the bourgeois process of ideological hegemony. Primary schools are the most important means (outside of the family) by which young children are socialized to accept prevailing social norms as "given". The curricula of primary schools are tightly regulated and controlled, and it is no accident that those who clamor for a return to teaching "traditional values" and the "three R's" are usually political and economic conservatives. For the most part, the educational system in the United States has two major social functions—to educate people in the social conventions of the society within they must live, and to provide the intellectual and technical abilities which will enable workers to perform their jobs after they graduate.

Of course, the most visible of the instruments of ideological hegemony in the United States is the mass media. The press and, even more so, the television, provide most Americans with nearly all of the information they will ever obtain about the world around them. By circumscribing the information we receive and the alternative viewpoints we are exposed to, the mass media can have a powerful influence on what people think, believe, and are willing to act upon.

Again, it should be stressed that this process of hegemony is not merely a system of overt propaganda, in which the media deliberately disseminates false information in order to mislead people. The process is much more subtle than that; it works, not by forcing others to adopt a particular point of view, but by limiting all potential outlooks to those consistent with current social relationships—a process referred to by Noam Chomsky as "manufacturing consent".

Bourgeois society makes the promise of "free speech and free press", but the economic realities of capitalism effectively eliminate these possibilities. In essence, capitalism guarantees freedom of press—to anyone who has the resources to own one. As Marx noted:

> The class which has the means of material production at its disposal, has control at the same time over the means of mental production, so that thereby, generally speaking, the ideas of those who lack the means of mental production are subject to it.

The mass media outlets may honestly believe that they are impartial and objective, but in reality they cannot change (or even consciously acknowledge) the fact that they are themselves large corporate entities, and are subject to all of the economic pressures which limit the viewpoints of any other large corporate entity. The existence of the media as an economic entity prevents it from viewing social reality in any framework that does not recognize or accept economic entities such as itself. The media cannot think in a non-corporate way precisely because they are corporations, and they are organized as corporations because without these economic resources, they would be unable to survive in a market economy.

The mass media also face inherent limitations because of the structure of their medium. Newspaper reporters are under stringent time limits and deadlines for submitting stories, and often have no time available to do a thorough job of research. As a result, most newspaper and magazine reporting consists simply of paraphrasing official information passed on by spokespersons and press releases. The smaller newspapers are in addition limited in their access to corporate or government officials, and thus are forced to depend upon merely repeating information which has been published by the larger media.

Television, from which most people receive their information, is even more severely limited. Television is heavily dependent upon visual images, and stories which cannot be presented effectively in pictures receive little attention. As a result, TV is forced to focus on visual events such as fires, disasters and sports. Many times, the image is more important than any actual information which is being communicated. A good example of this was the destruction of the space shuttle Challenger, when every TV network endless repeated the film footage of the disaster. In essence, the only information passed on for the first few hours was, "Something happened to the space shuttle, we don't know what, but here's what it looked like." Another good example was the CNN coverage of the First Gulf War, which looked more like a video game than coverage of a war. Watching CNN's antiseptic images, one may perhaps be forgiven for believing that nobody died.

TV is also severely limited in the amount of time it can spend on any one topic. The entire amount of words spoken in a half-hour newscast would not even fill the front page of a city newspaper. As a result, TV can provide only the most cursory information on any one topic, and is forced to avoid or oversimplify any news topic which cannot be reduced to a twenty-second "sound bite".

In essence, the ideological hegemony of the bourgeoisie can be viewed as a sort of "secular religion", in which existing social structures and relationships are deified and treated as an inescapable and unalterable part of reality. "The productions of the human brain," Marx writes, "appear as independent beings endowed with life, and entering into relations both with one another and with the human race." The capitalist's universe is dominated by the will, not of God, but of the Marketplace; the will of God was interpreted by the priests, but the will of the Marketplace is interpreted by the business owners. It is, Marx says, "a religion of everyday life".

It is in this web of ideological hegemony that we can see the secret of the bourgeoisie's elimination of dissent without the use of overt police force. As Bertell Ollman points out:

> Capitalism differs from all other oppressive systems in the amount and insidious character of its mystification, in the thoroughness with which it is integrated into all its life processes, and in the degree to which it requires mystification in order to survive (all other repressive systems rely far more on direct force).

This is not accomplished merely through manipulation or falsehood, however. Instead, it is accomplished through a process of gathering (and therefore presenting) all information within the context of an existing social framework, thus making it difficult for people to think thoughts which fall outside of that framework. As Ollman points out, the bourgeoisie's ideological justifications cannot be blatant propaganda or total lies, for if they were nobody would believe them and they would fail in their purpose:

> Bourgeois ideology offers explanations that are sufficiently in touch with the real world to permit life to go on and indeed for real progress to be made in some sectors. Though neither clear nor definite, there are limits, however, to what it can explain and what people will accept.

Because of the limited scope of bourgeois ideology, viewpoints always arise which reject the accepted socio-economic paradigm. In each area of ideological hegemony, insurgencies occasionally arise which challenge, either explicitly or implicitly, the accepted bourgeois world-view. In education, students have organized to demand a greater role in determining what is learned and how it is taught. In the media, a number of small "alternative" publications have attempted to expound new viewpoints, while the rise of "public-access TV", the Internet, and the proliferation of video cameras and computerized desktop publishing is increasing the ability of non-corporate sectors of society to disseminate their own point of view.

The ruling class, of course, is resisting all of these challenges. Sometimes, however, the capitalists themselves are forced to take actions which undermine their own ideological justifications: the New Deal, in opposition to the bourgeois religion of "laissez faire", produced a massive governmental intervention in the economy, in essence saving the marketplace from itself. Bertell Ollman writes:

> In the most recent period, the expanded economic role of the state . . . which was made necessary by the increasingly serious disruptions of the market, undercuts people's belief in the market as a natural phenomenon, and with it their acceptance of their place and rewards in life as facts of nature.

It is obvious that, if capitalist hegemony is to be undermined, it must be attacked in the intellectual sphere as well as the economic, racial, sexual and political spheres. To learn how to do this effectively, however, we must further examine the capitalist's "religion of everyday life". To help in this task, Marx introduced the concept of "alienation".

The word "alienation" appears throughout Marx's writings (particularly in the earlier, more "hegelian" works). Unfortunately, in the Leninist conception of Marxism, the concept of alienation has been almost completely lost (perhaps because Leninist "economic determinism" is itself a form of alienation).

Most people, even those who call themselves "Marxists", have little understanding of the concept. "The existing confusion over the term 'alienation'," writes Ollman, "has reached the point that many people use it to register simple dissatisfaction or, worse, feelings of social maladjustment."

To Marx, the term "alienation" had a very specific intention. It was used to signify a division which attempted to separate and treat as independent two things which were in reality inextricably united, and to give that artificial division a reality that it doesn't have.

In the Marxian world-view, things are seen in their totality as a series of interpenetrating dialectical relationships. That humans are, on the whole, unable to see this process of mutual interaction is due to the aims and goals of their social organization, which are based upon mutually antagonistic classes and social relationships.

The ruling class accomplishes this by constructing a system of abstracted human relationships which come to be viewed and accepted as "real". For instance, capitalist ideology declares that the economic circumstances of human beings are the result of the demands of an impersonal "Marketplace" — a marketplace which compels some people to do one thing and other people to do something else.

In reality, of course, it should be obvious that "the Marketplace" is merely an idealized abstraction which doesn't exist in reality — it is merely an idealized version of the actions of human individuals. Like all other idealized abstractions ("History" or "Human Nature"), "the Marketplace" is incapable of independent action and cannot "do" anything:

> History does nothing; it "possesses no wealth", it "wages no battles". It is humans, real humans, that do all that, that possess and fight; "history" is not a person apart, using humans as a means for its own particular aims; history is nothing other than the activity of humans pursuing their aims.

Marx compared this process of giving a human creation the ability to control human actions to that of a person who, one day, carves an idol from a piece of wood and then credits that idol with the attribute of having power over human beings, and falls down and worships it.

In nearly every case, this alienated ideological construction places humans in a passive role, and places a creation of human society in the active role. The marketplace is viewed as an entity that produces human actions, rather than the other way around. Marx compares this reversal to the Roman mythological figure Cacus, who steals oxen by dragging them off by the tail into a cave, making it appear as if the oxen have walked out of the cave rather than being forced into it.

The essence of alienation is that this abstraction comes to be viewed as an existing part of reality, as something which confronts human beings and forces them to act in certain ways. Marx writes:

> Their mutual relationship appears to the individuals themselves as something alien and autonomous, as an object. . . The social character of activity appears here as an alien object in relation to the individuals.

Alienation, Marx concluded, is the "consolidation of what we ourselves produce into an objective power over us, growing out of our control, thwarting our expectations, bringing to naught our calculations."

The Leninist economic determinists are unable to move beyond this alienation, since they view "economics" as a "thing" which exists apart from humans and which, through "natural laws", determines the actions of humans. The "scientific Marxists" fail to recognize that the concept of "economic laws" is as much an abstraction from human experience as are "history" or "the marketplace".

Marx never made this mistake. He asserted that humans are the source of everything in society—that all social relationships and institutions are the creations of humans, and that humans can consciously act to change any of these social relationships and institutions. "Though Marx generally organizes his findings around such non-human factors as the mode of production," Bertell Ollman points out, "his theory of alienation places the acting and acted-upon individual in the center of this account."

Engels puts it more simply: "Economics deals not with things but with relationships between persons, and, in the last resort, between classes."

By using alienating forms of ideology to present capitalist outlooks and institutions as unalterable "given" parts of reality, bourgeois hegemony prevents the rise of any system of thought which rejects these institutions, and makes any such system of thought seem unrealistic and "utopian". Ollman notes that such alienation has an effect on the development of socialist ideology among the working class: "Communism is seldom if ever opposed because one holds other values, but because it is said to be an unrealizable goal."

Nevertheless, Marx concluded, the separation of humans from each other through alienation could not continue forever. Humans are completely dependent upon each other for their existence, and this dependence necessitates direct face-to-face interaction, without the mediation of alienating abstractions. "Humans," writes Marx, "are in the most literal sense of the word a *zoon politikon*; not only a social animal, but an animal which can develop into an individual only in society":

> The real active orientation of humans to themselves as a species-being, or their manifestation as a real species-being (i.e., as human beings), is only possible by their really bringing out of themselves all the powers that are their as species beings.
> Only in community with others has each individual the means of cultivating his gifts in all directions; only in community, therefore, is personal freedom possible.

"By 'community'," Ollman adds, "Marx has in mind a sincere and multi- faceted relationship binding each individual to everyone else in society."

Bourgeois ideology, of course, asserts the opposite — that people are "rugged individuals" who are most free when their activities are isolated from everyone else. The capitalist concept of atomistic, self-supporting individuals, however, ignores reality. Humans cannot live independently from other humans. Not only are they dependent economically on what other humans have produced, but their very existence is dependent on a sexual and family bond between humans, which cannot take place without a social structure.

Direct face-to-face bonds between people are made difficult in capitalism, which uses alienating social institutions to mediate between inter-personal ties. The producer and the consumer, for example, rarely relate to each other directly as human beings in capitalism—they can only relate impersonally through the marketplace. "Such direct bonds," Ollman says, "can only come into existence after all artificial barriers to the mutual involvement of people have been torn down."

In order for alienation to be overcome and for people to relate as true social individuals, the alienating structures of capitalism must be torn down. Among these alienating constructions is capitalist economics, with its concept of impersonal economic laws.

Marx, therefore, saw communist revolution not so much as an economic program or an ideology, but as a necessary consequence of and prerequisite for the transcendence of human alienation. This transcendence, he pointed out, was only possible within the framework of the abolition of private property and the wage system:

> The positive transcendence of private property as the appropriation of human life is, therefore, the positive transcendence of all alienation—that is to say, the return of man from religion, family, state, etc., to his human, i.e., social mode of existence.
> Communism as the positive transcendence of private property as human self-estrangement; and therefore as the real appropriation of the human essence by and for humans; communism therefore as the complete return of people to themselves as a social (i.e., human) being—a return accomplished consciously and embracing the entire wealth of previous development. This communism, as fully developed materialism, equals humanism, and as fully developed humanism, equals naturalism; it is the genuine resolution of the conflict between human and nature and between human and human.

Thus, a society of freely-interacting human beings is not possible until the alienating structures of capitalism are destroyed. Those who see Marxism as simply an ideology or a socio-economic system are missing the point. As Marx himself writes:

> Communism is not for us a state of affairs which is to be established, an ideal to which reality will have to adjust itself. We call communism the real movement which abolishes the present state of things. The conditions of this movement result from the premises now in existence.

Marxism is concerned with the destruction of alienating social institutions and the creation of new, humanistic relationships in their place. And, as we have seen, this is the same goal of every other radical social movement—to put social institutions under the free control of the humans involved, and to have a society of freely-interacting human beings.

Economics is, therefore, not the only sphere in which alienating social structures prevent free human action. Indeed, every social relationship which we have examined in this book is at root a relationship between groups and classes of people, mediated by a social construction that appears to "cause" these interactions. Just as the classes of worker and owner are forced to relate to each other through the social institution of the economic marketplace, the classes of men and women must relate to each other through the social institution of the family, racial and national classes are alienated from each other by artificial national boundaries, and those who wield political power are insulated from those who have none through the institution of the state.

Each of these non-economic class relationships developed into alienating institutions in the same way as economics. Ollman says;

> In each instance, the other half of a severed relation, carried by a social dynamic of its own, progresses through a series of reforms in a direction away from its beginning in man. Eventually, it attains an independent life, that is, takes on "needs" which the individual is then forced to satisfy, and the original connection is all but obliterated.

Bourgeois hegemony maintains the social institutions under which each class victim of alienation reproduces the conditions for this oppression by their own actions. The workers can only live by selling their labor power to bosses in the marketplace, and thus must accept the social institutions of wage labor, private ownership and exchange which reinforce the marketplace, and thus continues their own exploitation. Women must relate to men through family and gender roles, and thus accept and reinforce these roles for the next generation of women. Environmentalists who criticize industrial pollution must nevertheless operate within the framework of industrialism, and thus insure that industrialization will continue and cause more environmental damage.

This process of ideological alienation is reinforced in turn by the interlocking system of bourgeois social relationships, which reinforce and propagate each other. This web of ideological and institutional restraints, this network of bourgeois hegemony, is how the capitalist class stays alive in a world of lopsided social relationships.

Since all spheres of human society — economic, sexual, racial, national — are alienating and tend to reproduce each other, the total system of bourgeois hegemony can only be broken by attacking each institution. Just as economic alienation can only be broken by an "economic class consciousness" (i.e., by an understanding of the relationships of humans to the means of production), racial alienation can only be broken by "racial class consciousness" (an understanding of the relationship between differing ethnic classes), and sexual liberation demands "gender class consciousness" (an understanding of the way men as a class relate to women as a class).

Each oppressed class must develop a full picture of its social position and how this position is maintained and reproduced. Once it is seen clearly that all of these repressive social institutions and relationships are socially-produced — *not* inevitable natural "givens" — the possibility can be raised of changing these social relations and institutions through conscious willful actions. In other words, the possibility arises of revolution.

Conclusion: Counter-Hegemony

There is, we have noted, a tendency among critics of existing society to look at the social structures which most directly affect them. Radical feminists, for instance, examine the relationship between genders. Anarchists examine issues of power and control. Latino, African-American, Native American and other racial or ethnic activists focus on these national relationships. Traditional Marxists and Leninists focus on the interaction of economic classes.

Each of these particular outlooks is, we have seen, incomplete and misleading. In a real functioning society of human beings, these "sub-structures" interpenetrate to reinforce and reproduce each other. In the workplace, an economic struggle takes place between capitalist and worker. At the same time, an authority struggle rages between employee and employer, while racial and gender struggles break out over racial and sexual issues.

In the educational institutions, these same struggles occur. The children of wealthy people are trained to assume roles of authority and leadership, while those from poorer families receive "vocational training", and learn to accept the authority and discipline of the workplace. Women are conditioned for "female" roles, while everybody is socialized into acceptable sexual, racial and national roles.

In the nuclear family, some are dependent on the wages and income received by others, and this economic relationship reinforces the authority the wage earner holds over the rest. Women are assigned sexual and family roles to play, and men are assigned quite different roles. Unwritten rules concerning friendships, playmates and marriages reinforce the "socially accepted" relationships between families of different ethnicity, religion or class.

Some social critics have spent most of their time discussing which of these various forms of exploitation and repression appeared "first". Engels gave the accepted "Marxist view" on the matter when he wrote, in *The Origin of the Family, Private Property and the State*, that divisions along gender lines were the first "class" distinctions. The whole matter is, however, a pointless debate that does nothing to help us understand and change the actual conditions of today. To do that, we need to look at how present social relationships interact without worrying about which was chronologically "first".

Other theorists have wasted their time and effort in debate over "whose oppression is the most oppressive", and therefore which liberation struggle is the "most important". This is another useless exercise, but one that has a fairly simple solution—the most oppressive relationship is the one you feel most oppressed by.

Prime offenders in both of these categories have been the traditional Leninist "economic determinists". Contrary to the assertions of the Communists, however, the source of the bourgeois class's power is not merely that it controls capital and thus places workers in a disadvantaged economic position. The ruling class's power comes from the fact that it is able to implement and reproduce a number of alienating social relationships which safeguard its position of privilege, and that it is able to defend these social relationships from the attempts of the oppressed to change them.

The primary sanction for people to stay within their assigned roles is "negative reinforcement"; by venturing outside of "accepted" social roles, people cut themselves off from various social needs and desires. For instance, a worker is not forced to labor at a wage job and thus produce surplus value for the capitalist, but if she doesn't she receives no wage income and thus cannot buy the necessities of life. A person who refuses to accept the established norms for family roles will not be able to marry and have a family.

The study of non-economic relationships explains how the capitalist system is able to maintain itself without resorting to physical coercion. These alienating relationships, between men and women, between order-giver and order-taker, between straight and gay — all serve to condition people to accept the bourgeois order of things as a natural, inevitable and inescapable part of reality.

Through such a system of hegemony, bourgeois society succeeds in compelling people to fit themselves into the accepted roles, and thus to modify their own behavior in ways that serve to protect and propagate these social institutions.

However, since social relationships in bourgeois society are geared towards serving the needs of the ruling elite rather than social needs, fitting oneself into the acceptable roles often means that some individual social needs remain unfulfilled. Any unmet needs, whether the need for shared decision-making, for free sexual roles, or for national self-determination, can become a potential source of people who reject bourgeois society's established social roles. Whenever alienation is overcome, and existing social institutions are seen to be human creations rather than unchanging conditions of life, a radical consciousness results.

Furthermore, the desire to alter one set of social relationships can bring with it the possibility of seeing the limitations of others, and of substituting an entirely new social structure (one that is better-suited to the needs of freely-interacting individuals) for the existing one. In other words, it brings the possibility of a *revolutionary* consciousness.

The realization that a revolutionary consciousness may result from a number of different social conflicts opens bourgeois society to a unified attack. In essence, revolutionaries find that they must undermine all existing social relationships and put new social relationships in their place—the bourgeois cultural hegemony must be replaced by a new counter-hegemony.

The tactics of the traditional Marxists and Leninists are entirely unsuited for this task. No alliance of progressive forces can be maintained while any one element of this alliance continues to view itself as "more basic" or "more important" than the others. Inevitably, the rest of the movement will fall under the control of the strongest element, and the necessary broad-based movement will collapse. Only a wide-ranging social movement based upon autonomous but complementary components can hope to defeat bourgeois hegemony.

Such is the problem with Leninism and "scientific Marxism". By asserting that the economic struggle between workers and capitalists is the "most important", traditional Marxists ignore (or, worse, attempt to take over) the other struggles for human liberation—anti-sexist, anti-racist, etc. By asserting, for example, that racism exists only to serve the needs of capitalism, and keeps racial minorities in an inferior social position so they can be economically exploited, the "economic determinists" ignore the fact that the reverse is also true— capitalism exists to serve racism, and racists use unequal economic relationships as a way of keeping racial minorities weak and powerless. It is true that economic factors have a large impact on the structures of racism, but it is equally true that racism has a large impact on the structures of the economy.

Even in the "economic battleground" of the workplace, the conflict between workers and owners is not merely economic, not solely a haggling over wages and hours. Workers also organize and fight for such non-economic goals as decision-making power, the ability to freely express their own creativity at work, and even the ability to have fun on the job. When workers at a plant strike to protest sexual harassment on the job, or to demand day care centers at the workplace, or even the right to play checkers in the lunch room, they are fighting for more than mere economics; they are fighting for the right to determine their own destiny and to have control over their own circumstances. This fight extends into every sphere of bourgeois society, and forms the basis for every anti-bourgeois social movement.

Some social critics have begun to recognize the need for coordinated action against the ruling elite, and have attempted to unify the analyses of different social movements. The eco-feminists, for instance, combine an environmental and a feminist analysis in their programs, while the anarcho-communists enhance a Marxian economic analysis through an anti-authoritarian critique.

If bourgeois society is to fall, however, it must be attacked simultaneously on all of these fronts by a concerted, multi-faceted revolutionary front. While all of the various social dissident movements — feminists, anarchists, environmentalists, gay activists, socialists — must carry on their own struggles under their own direction, they must also grow together to form a cohesive movement with complementary goals. Bourgeois society is not an edifice with a "cornerstone" which, if removed, causes the whole structure to collapse. Rather, it is a teepee — remove any one of the supporting poles, and the others will prop it up. Remove *all* the poles, and a new structure can be built in its place.

Bourgeois hegemony can only be replaced through a socialist viewpoint; not merely "socialist" in the sense that the economic process must be controlled socially rather than by individual owners, but "socialist" in the sense that it is the conscious desire and activity of all members of society. The revolution must grow to encompass, not merely the economic means of production, but the entire mode of social life, including its familial, sexual, racial, national, gender and authority roles. The entire process of humanity's interaction with itself and with its surroundings must be brought under the willfully-directed control of the totality of that society. It must be truly *social*-ist.

Such a socialist revolution can only consist of a series of interlocking "counter-hegemonies". To combat capitalist hegemony in the workplace, it is necessary to replace the institution of the marketplace with direct cooperative production and exchange. To combat the hegemonies of men over women and straight over gay, sexist and heterosexist institutions must be replaced by freely-chosen personal relationships. To overthrow the hegemony of the nuclear family, free sexual relationships are a necessity. To end the destruction of the natural environment, industry must be transformed from a force of and for itself into the consciously-controlled tools of human beings. To break the grip of alienating ideology, education must be turned from a institution for training and socializing people into a personal learning experience. In every case, free and conscious personal relationships must replace the existing social restrictions.

The model for this revolutionary approach can be seen in the "Movement" of the 1960's. In the space of a dozen years, a dazzling variety of organizations arose, including the anti-war movement, the civil rights/Black Power movement, the American Indian Movement and La Raza, the New Left, the hippie counter-culture, the women's liberation movement, the gay/lesbian movement and the ecology movement. All of these were facets of a single "proto-social-ist" organization, a multi-faceted movement that fought for human liberation and self-determination, and fought against alienation and social fragmentation. The Movement concerned itself with questions of race, sexuality, psychology, education, consciousness and education, to an extent that shocked the ossified "Old Left". For a brief moment, the entire existing sphere of social reality came under critical scrutiny, and was found wanting.

In practice, however, the 1960's "social-ist" movement was crippled by several factors. Its various component groups were atomistic and isolated from each other, and lacked a coordinated plan to launch an all-out assault on bourgeois culture. The Movement was also crippled by its "national" character; although counter-culture movements appeared in virtually every industrialized country (including the Soviet Bloc), there was little international cooperation between them. Finally, nowhere was the Movement able to develop a significant following among the majority of workers. Deprived of a major source of power, the Movement was too weak to be able to defend itself against the repression launched against it by the bourgeoisie.

In the first years of the 21st century, the situation appears to share similarities with the '60's, with some important differences. As in the '60's, the 2000's have seen a period of reactionary policies being challenged by a growing movement for social justice. In the 1960's, however, a surging economy made it possible for the ruling class to "buy off" protest movements with promises of reform. Today, the faltering position of the United States in the world economy are causing increasing discontent while at the same time limiting the ability of the elites to deal with protest.

The trade union labor movement, which was at the height of its power in the 1960's, is now weak and disorganized. The budding "industrial democracy" movement, however, may prove to be the initial stage of a new militant labor movement, one that will challenge the capitalists as well as the labor union bureaucrats, and bring rank-and-file control to the workplace. Combined with a new resurgence in the feminist, gay liberation, African-American and ecology movements, a militant rank-and-file labor movement can provide strength for a wide-ranging social movement that will challenge the very structure of modern capitalist society.

It is possible, then, that the 2000's may provide the mass movement for which the 1960's were simply a "dress rehearsal." If the social justice movement is able to coalesce into a wide-ranging, coordinated entity, and if bourgeois hegemony comes under serious attack on every front, the existing social order may not be able to stand up to the challenge. Human institutions and relations may at last come under conscious human control.